The Word
Of the Cross

The Word
Of the Cross

WATCHMAN NEE
Translated from the Chinese

Christian Fellowship Publishers, Inc.
New York

ISBN 0-935008-80-2

Available from the Publishers at:

11515 Allecingie Parkway
Richmond, Virginia 23235

PRINTED IN U.S.A.

TRANSLATOR'S PREFACE

In his first letter to the Corinthians the apostle Paul wrote: "And I, brethren, when I came unto you, came not with excellency of speech or of wisdom, proclaiming to you the testimony of God. For I determined not to know anything among you, save Jesus Christ, and him crucified" (2.1-2). This same spirit overshadowed the life and ministry of Watchman Nee. From his early Christian years he embraced the cross of Christ and proclaimed the Christ of the cross. He never moved away from this foundation throughout his many years of faithful ministry.

This present volume is comprised of his early writings from the years 1922–1927.* Though young in the Lord, he was given much because he loved much. His first love towards the Lord was pure and warm, and his grasp of the truth was firm and solid. In reading these writings it uplifts our hearts and deepens our faith.

The readers will find this book divided into three parts. Part One, Musings Under the Cross, unveils the innermost thoughts of a man in first love. Part Two is The Word of the Cross which lays a firm foundation of our faith. Part Three is on Faith and other related subjects that deal with the subjective aspects of the Christian life. The combination of all three parts offers up a balanced picture of normal Christian living.

May the Lord who fed the multitudes with five loaves and two fish feed us today with this small collection.

---

*All were originally composed and published in Chinese but have been translated afresh into English for this present volume.

CONTENTS

PART ONE

MUSINGS UNDER THE CROSS

1 | My Spiritual Journey*

Once I dwelt "in the tents of wickedness" (Ps. 84.10), "walked according to the course of this world, according to the prince of the powers of the air, of the spirit that now worketh in the sons of disobedience" (Eph. 2.2), and "lived in the lusts of [my] flesh, doing the desires of the flesh and of the mind, and [was] by nature [a child] of wrath, even as the rest" (Eph. 2.3).

But I then heard "a great high priest, who had passed through the heavens, Jesus the Son of God" (Heb. 4.14) and who is building a mansion for me, for "in my Father's house," He said, there "are many mansions" (John 14.2).

I was once utterly hopeless, just "as it is written, There is none righteous, no, not one; there is none that understandeth, there is none that seeketh after

---

*This article was written by the author less than two years after he was saved and was published in *Spiritual Light* magazine, December 1921. —*Translator*

God; they have all turned aside, they are together become unprofitable; there is none that doeth good, no, not so much as one: their throat is an open sepulchre; with their tongues they have used deceit: the poison of asps is under their lips: whose mouth is full of cursing and bitterness: their feet are swift to shed blood; destruction and misery are in their ways; and the way of peace have they not known: there is no fear of God before their eyes. Now we know that what things soever the law saith, it speaketh to them that are under the law; that every mouth may be stopped, and all the world may be brought under the judgment of God" (Rom. 3.10-19). So I made inquiry: "Jesus saith unto them, Believe ye that I am able to do this? They say unto him, Yea, Lord" (Matt. 9.28).

Thus I met Him at "a place called Golgotha, that is to say, The place of a skull" (Matt. 27.33). And what He said to me was: "if thou shalt confess with thy mouth Jesus as Lord, and shalt believe in thy heart that God raised him from the dead, thou shalt be saved: for with the heart man believeth unto righteousness; and with the mouth confession is made unto salvation" (Rom. 10.9-10).

Now I am walking as having "purged out the old leaven, that [I] may be a new lump, even as [I am] unleavened. For [my] passover also hath been sacrificed, even Christ" (1 Cor. 5.7). I have "received the gift of the Holy Spirit" (Acts 2.38) who dwells within me.

I today journey in "the way, and the truth, and the life" (John 14.6). I now see God, for "he that hath seen me," said Jesus, "hath seen the Father" (John 14.9).

I found at last the house that I had long sought after—"a building from God, a house not made with hands, eternal in the heavens" (2 Cor. 5.1). This house has but one door, for I see that "by me," declared Jesus, "if any man enter in, he shall be saved" (John 10.9). I now realize the truth of Jesus' saying: "knock, and it shall be opened unto you" (Matt. 7.7).

The house where I today live has a music room— "Glory ye in his holy name: let the heart of them rejoice that seek Jehovah. Seek ye Jehovah and his strength; seek his face evermore" (Ps. 105.3-4). It has a conversation chamber—where I am to "pray without ceasing" (1 Thess. 5.17). It likewise has a reading room—for "examining the scriptures daily, [to see] whether these things were so" (Acts 17.11). And it has a lecture hall—"To the weak I became weak, that I might gain the weak: I am become all things to all men, that I may by all means save some" (1 Cor. 9.22). And finally my bedroom is "Jesus' breast" (John 13.25).

My present lodging is where "I have been crucified with Christ; and it is no longer I that live, but Christ liveth in me: and that life which I now live in the flesh I live in faith, the faith which is in the Son of God, who loved me, and gave himself up for me" (Gal. 2.20). And my address is "in the heavenly places" (Eph. 2.6). Whenever you visit me in the spirit of "Blessed is the man that heareth me [that is, heareth Wisdom, which is Christ], watching daily at my gates, waiting at the posts of my doors" (Prov. 8.34), you will find not only me but also my fellow saints. Take heed to what the servant says, "Come; for all things are now ready" (Luke 14.17).

"Then we that are alive, that are left, shall together with them be caught up in the clouds, to meet the Lord in the air: and so shall we ever be with the Lord" (1 Thess. 4.17). After these words are fulfilled, I shall have my home where "I saw thrones, and they sat upon them: and I saw the souls of them that had been beheaded for the testimony of Jesus, and for the word of God, and such as worshipped not the beast, neither his image, and received not the mark upon their forehead and upon their hand; and they lived, and reigned with Christ a thousand years. The rest of the dead lived not until the thousand years should be finished. This is the first resurrection. Blessed and holy is he that hath part in the first resurrection: over these the second death hath no power; but they shall be priests of God and of Christ, and shall reign with him a thousand years" (Rev. 20.4-6). And the song I sing shall be ". . . a new song, saying, Worthy art thou to take the book, and to open the seals thereof: for thou wast slain, and did purchase unto God with thy blood men of every tribe, and tongue, and people, and nation" (Rev. 5.9).

Not very long afterwards I along with my beloved ones shall move into "a new heaven and a new earth: for the first heaven and the first earth are passed away; and the sea is no more" (Rev. 21.1). For "according to his promise, we look for new heavens and a new earth, wherein dwelleth righteousness" (2 Peter 3.13). "Wherefore," at that time, the word—"if any man is in Christ, he is a new creature: the old things are passed away; behold, they are become new" (2 Cor. 5.17)— shall be fully realized, and I shall gloriously experience the truth of this word: "Rejoice in the Lord always: again I will say, Rejoice" (Phil. 4.4).

In such manner had the saints of old made their own spiritual journey. Yet these lines also represent what I myself have experienced and earnestly expect. Indeed, in writing the very last section, I was beside myself with *joyful* tears. But I suppose you who are saved have the same feeling towards the return of the Lord Jesus. Those who are cleansed by the blood of Jesus are naturally optimistic towards life. But where will you who have not the assurance of being saved spend eternal death? Please consider!

2 | Musings Under the Cross

Translator's Note: Some background knowledge may help the reader to understand better these musings under the cross which are to follow. A work of God had begun in Foochow, China in the year 1923. In laboring together with fellow workers, Watchman Nee as a young man learned many spiritual lessons. He himself acknowledged later the following year: "I confess that in this year and a half I have learned life's most precious lesson. Formerly my mind was filled with imagination, but God used different circumstances to lead me into spiritual reality, into the knowledge of the meaning of the cross." He also shared: "In the years from 1921 to 1923 there were revivals in many places. Many maintained that since these revival meetings brought souls to the Lord we ought to concentrate on this type of meeting. But the Lord had shown me that His will was to have all the saved souls stand together on the ground of unity so as to represent the local church in the testimony of God."

"Unfortunately," continued brother Nee, "some fellow workers did not endorse this concept. I diligently searched the book of Acts and was fully convinced that God's will is to establish churches in various localities. I had clear light on this will of God. Due to such revelation, problems arose. Those fellow workers who had not seen this light held a different view regarding the focus of our work. Thus it created conflict among us. They felt we should actively be engaged in preaching the gospel and working on revival, for these brought in visible results. But the Lord showed me that His heart was in establishing local churches. This was my burden. All the other works became secondary. . . . The revelation the Lord gave me was very clear. In the near future He would raise up local churches in China's larger and smaller cities. Even now, as I close my eyes, that vision appears at once before me."

It was for this reason that brother Nee suffered a great deal during this critical year of 1923. And thus it helps to explain these musings under the cross, which he recorded throughout that year. They unveil his first love for the Lord, his loyalty to the vision God had given him, and his inward and outward sufferings.*

1. It has not been long since I believed in the Lord [which had occurred on 29 April 1920]. It was only

---

*The "musings" which now follow in this chapter appeared, as it were, in serial form in the latter issues (nos. 16-21) of *Spiritual Light* for the year 1923. And thus their contents were published in this Christian magazine not long after the author's experience of them, the last of which (Point 5) having been dated 28 December 1923. Point 6, comprising in itself a number of musings, was written shortly afterwards to serve as a concluding word to the entire series, all of which were composed at Jade Forest Hall Cottage, Foochow. —*Translator* three years and one month ago [which means this Point 1. was set down in late May 1923]. There is not much spiritual experience one can talk about, though in God's grace I have been shown a little. I would rather hide this as my personal secret, lest in telling it to people I be misunderstood. For I would suffer painfully should the name of the Lord suffer loss as a result. However, the day of the Lord's return is imminent. The day of us believers returning home is not far away. Will not my fellow travelers have the same feeling as I have? With this in mind and with the Lord's permission, I write this paper to encourage my fellow "strangers and sojourners" in seeking together Christian perfection. What is presented may be taken as some Scripture readings or as fragmentary spiritual experiences (or both). These are but songs sung along the pathway of cross-bearing.

"Whom have I in heaven but thee? And there is none upon earth that I desire besides thee" (Ps. 73.25). Last year when I read this, I could not respond heartily. I could not say this word from my heart. This was because my love for my friend was so intense that though I loved the Lord my love was divided. Many times the Lord urged me to forsake all and obey Him, but I could not. Later on He showed me that if I really desired to be greatly used by Him I must fully obey, or else I would not be filled with the Holy Spirit. I tried to bargain with the Lord, saying that having a lover was an excellent thing in life. Why should He insist on my spending this life in loneliness? But He deemed such love as not originating from Him, therefore it was but worldly affection.

February 13th [1923] came. The love of Christ filled my heart, and I surrendered all. I prayed: "O Lord! Hereafter I will not consider myself as mine. For Your sake I am willing to forsake all. I am Yours, be it life or death. O Lord, whom have I in heaven but Thee? And there is none upon earth that I desire besides Thee. The love of Christ is eternal and never fails. Hence, I should love Him forever and ever." Henceforth, each time I think of how the Lord had forsaken all for me, though I too have forsaken all for Him, yet the all I have forsaken for Him is so much less than a millionth of *His* all. O Lord! Keep this consecrated heart of mine.

"Thou didst cause men to ride over our heads" (Ps. 66.12). O Lord! I am open to Your giving others carriage to ride. I am willing to lie in dust and be an unnoticed, unknown servant. Though I be so debased as to have men ride over my head, I am satisfied if only I have You.

"For the help of his countenance" (Ps. 42.5). O Lord! Although lately I have been pressed by circumstances and my future is dark, my course is enlightened by Your smiling face. Even if my whole being is cast down and disquieted, my strength in walking is renewed with just a smile from You. I do not care how people treat me; what I do care about is Your smiling face. All who do the will of God do not lose heart. What other helps do we look for since we already have the Lord's approval and the help of His countenance?

If the thing that I pray for is the Lord's will and He wants me to have it, then He must work towards my having it. In case it is not His will for me to have it, then what use is it for me to even have it?

If I am in the will of the Lord, I must be joyful. If I am not, O Lord, place me in Your will.

"Jesus did not trust himself unto them, for that he knew all men" (John 2.24). God is strong and faithful; I naturally can commit myself to Him. But how about me? Will the Lord commit himself to me? Were I able to know human beings, I would never commit myself to their praises. I only desire the praise from God (see 1 Cor. 4.5).

Valiant men keep the doors (see 1 Chron. 26.1,6-9). The Church of God is in great need of big talents for small uses.

"Jehovah spake . . . saying, . . . he was jealous with my jealousy" (Num. 25.11). On 7 May 1923 I said, "O Lord, my heart is in sympathy with You. Whatever You are jealous for, I too am jealous. Whatever You love, I also love."

For the sake of Christ, Paul "count[ed] all things to be loss" (Phil. 3.8a). He not only counted all as loss, He actually "suffered the loss of all things" (v.8b). Our offering to the Lord ought not be a lip-offering or a mind-offering; rather, it must be from the heart and factual.

"Paul, a servant of Jesus Christ" (Rom. 1.1). Formerly he was the honor student of Gamaliel, born among a chosen people of God, prominent among the Pharisees, a Roman citizen by right of birth, and having in his hand prized privileges and influence. Later Paul constantly traveled on the road, frequently came down with infirmities, and bore in his body the scars of scourging. He was looked upon by the world as a plague and was despised as "the filth of the world" and "the offscouring of all things" (1 Cor. 4.10). Often he was forsaken and spent his days in desolate loneliness. He was quite familiar with hunger and cold. He worked till dawn making tents. What a Saul he was before: but now he called himself "Paul, a servant of Jesus Christ [the despised Nazarene]." He knew the preciousness of Jesus Christ, for whom he forsook all things.

O Lord! Although I had many opportunities to be Your servant and at the same time have the praise and glory of the world, I would rather be forsaken, going outside the camp to suffer with you [see Heb. 13.13].

2. "Suffering" is "glory." Having suffered with the Lord, we shall be glorified with Him. Suffering is future glory; and glory is present suffering.

At first I sought for ease and comfort; but when my love for the Lord became intense I sought for labor. Now I seek neither ease nor labor. If the Lord considers me qualified to suffer a little with Him, then let me suffer according to His good pleasure. I know laboring with the Lord is both joyful and sweet.

I have learned the lesson that in working with people, whatever matter it may be, once an opinion is raised, not to insist any more. If people do not listen, retreat into prayer. Bear all things for Christ's sake. Recall how patient is God. Why can I not be patient too? Let God work out His purpose without my voice.

To the Lord always say "Yes." Whatever the Lord

may command me to do, I should say "Yes, Lord." "Not my will but Thy will." This is the secret of victory.

I frequently recall how in past days I was surrounded with earthly friends, and had position, taste and ambition. How great and how lovely it all was! Even now, such recollection tempts me to draw back. "O Lord, enable me for Your sake to forget the things which are behind and stretch forward to the things that are before." [See Phil. 3.13.]

Paul regards us as soldiers of Christ (2 Tim. 2.3-4). When a soldier goes to the front, he is ready to die. If he is wounded, this is no surprise. "O Lord! Make me a believer who counts not life as dear. When my affection is hurt by the world, let me remember that this is expected of believers." It is normal for a soldier to die; it is exceptional for him to live. Why then should we soldiers of Christ be exceptions? A soldier looks for victory; a general is made out of wounds.

In order to serve the Lord, I still remain single. Though I am among men, yet I have been separated from the world. Casting aside my education, forsaking my friends, I travel far and wide beneath the scorching sun to spread the name of the Lord. Rarely do I have sufficient rest and adequate food; I also at times lay by in sick bed. Lacking any help, what do I have except the veiled smile of the Lord's face? On behalf of the Lord, my life here on earth is full of tribulations. During windy mornings and moonlit nights, I cannot help but pity myself if I fall into thinking of myself instead of my Lord. As I recall the past and recount the present, it is hard for me to console myself. Many times I shed tears. "O Lord!" once cried out Peter, "pity thyself" (Matt. 16.22 paraphrased). Jesus in this chapter spoke of going to Jerusalem to suffer. Peter counseled Him with these words, but the Lord judged it as counsel from Satan. "O Lord! From now on deliver me from self-pity. May I never console this useless self. Whether I live or die I am the Lord's. Let me do Thy will to please Thee."

Were you ever alone? Why seek for intimate friends and sigh? Do you not know that in the depth of Jesus' heart there is deep love and unspeakable peace?

O Lord! I am now wholly Yours. Work out Your will in me relentlessly. Have no regard of my discomfort. As long as Your will is done, my heart is satisfied.

O Lord! I am now in need. I gladly accept it so long as this does not disgrace Your name. O my heart, do not be anxious. The Lord knows when is the best time to supply. He is never late. So, rest in Him.

Jesus is the eternal bread. No one both eats the bread and thanks the bread. So let me serve according to the will of God and accept not the praise of men. Let me hide in the Lord. "O Lord! How my heart longs for my home, my country. Come quickly."

I sojourn temporarily in this world. Soon I shall return home—home, sweet home. How joyful is the way to home. Every day I am ready to hear the voice, "Come up hither" (see Rev. 4.1, 11.12). In case misfortune comes upon me, a coffin is enough in sending me to the dust. Even if there be no coffin, what does it matter? Though lonesome on earth, I have the Lord; so I have nothing to be discontented about. Despising the judgment of the world, my heart is satisfied with the Lord's smiling face. "My future is dark, O Lord! Yet with Your one smile it is transformed into light."

Thank the Lord! Today is past, so my homegoing is a day nearer. The coming of the Lord is also a day closer. O Lord Jesus, come quickly.

This morning the Lord calls me to serve Him this day. May the Lord keep me in His love throughout the day and may I be lost to myself.

Formerly I thought my nothingness was a hindrance to God's work; now, though, unless I am nothing I cannot work for Him at all. Hereafter I am an empty vessel in the Lord's hand to be used by Him. Yet even in this regard, Satan subtly comes to work on this nothingness. He tempts me to boast of my nothingness, to make me think of my lackluster nothingness as something to be enjoyed and be proud of! And thus my nothingness is no longer nothing! O Lord, such enjoyment is Satan's counterfeit. May I be abased and the Lord be exalted. May all glory be unto You, Lord. Amen.

3. O Lord! Today two paths lie before me. I do not know which is Yours and which is not Yours. Please show me Your way. O Lord! If I am too big to fit into Your plan, cut me down that I may meet Your will. Or if I am too small to fulfill Your plan, enlarge me that I may accomplish Your purpose.

O Lord! In the past I was a sinner. I thank You, for in Christ Jesus You have forgiven my sins. Make me as holy as You wish me to be.

I am a very sensitive person. Whenever I encounter something, I am either deeply anxious or exceedingly happy over it. Oftentimes I walk to and fro in "Ele-phant Hill" (that is my temporary earthly address) and commune with the Lord. When I think on my life, I frequently shed tears. If it is not for the Lord, I would not be in such a situation. I love to study. Once I vowed to pursue after the best education I could ever get. And now in order to love my Jesus and serve Him somewhat, I desert my education. How my tears wet my shirt as I reflect on this during my crossing the Ming River. Yet at that time, in view of the pleasant environment and the distinctive love of my Lord, I quickly burst out laughing. "O Lord! I now offer to You both tears and smiles. For my tears and my smiles are Yours. Whether I shed a drop of tear or flash a wink of smile, it is all for You. If Your heart is glad, I am glad and smile. If Your heart is sorrowful, I too am sorrowful and weep." From now on, I am determined not to shed tears over my life situation nor to be joyful over my environment. Whatever may come, I will first enquire where the Lord's heart is and how He will deal with it. "O Lord! Is Your heart joyful? If You are not happy, I too am unhappy. Is Your heart sorrowful? If You are not sorrowful, neither am I."

Last year [1922] came an opportunity for me to go to America to study in the Moody Bible Institute. It stirred my buried wish. It did not happen because it was not the Lord's will. (The will of the Lord is always the best.) This year in July, I traveled with my two friends, Faithful Luke and Simon Meek. When we talked about our mutual friends in America, my heart was again stirred. That very evening I met a lady mis-sionary, and she again invited me to go to the States to study. "O Lord! Now my all is Yours. Whatever you desire of me, that I will do. Whatever You do not want, I will not do. For You I live; for You I die. My hands are on the plow; how, then, dare I look back at the world? [Luke 9.62] O Lord! I look at You and seek You only."

I wrote on the first page of my Bible, saying that this book speaks of the One whom I have not seen yet love (1 Peter 1.8). Hence I love to read it.

Though Satan may block me, yet he cannot stop me.

Dear reader, is the heavenly path rugged and all ascending? The answer is, Yes. Is it so throughout the days? The answer is, From night to day.

21 October 1923. "O Lord! My heart rejoices. Formerly I rejoiced because I had something to offer You. Today my heart is exceedingly joyful because I have nothing more to offer. And the reason? Because, Lord, all are Yours."

"O Lord! Do I know how to praise You? What I sing is 'Your praise'."

"O Lord! Formerly I was satisfied in You, now I know You are my satisfaction. Having You, I want no other person, no other thing, no other event."

"O Lord! Today I am again being misunderstood. I ask You to enable me at this moment to love the person more who misunderstood me. I thank You! For You have never once misunderstood me."

"O precious Lord! It does not matter if people do not love me, for You always love me. People often misjudge my motive, but You always know. Let not people love me unless they love me with Your love."

"My Lord, You always love me! Let nothing stand between You and me. I will come to You, Lord, without interruption, will come to commune with You heart to heart. Worldly affection and glory tend to separate us. May You draw me that I may come closer to You."

On 23 October the Lord said to me: "Unless you count My order as most important, you are not able to save souls for Me." Doing God's will is top priority; saving many souls is not a big issue. "O Lord! Suppose You order me to enter into Your field and labor for ten years without rescuing a single soul; I can be fully contented, for I have done Your will. I want faithfulness, not fruit." Since the Lord apportions the field to me, I will not go elsewhere even if I may save more souls. "O Lord! I will not go to the place of my preference, but go to the field to which You sent me."

4. In the morning of 28 October 1923 I prayed: "O Lord, I now appreciate Your suffering (yet only a tiny bit of it). I went to the country place. I felt nobody knew me. No one sympathized with me. But You came from heaven to earth. Your loneliness, Your solitude . . . is beyond description. I now know Your sufferings somewhat. I thank You! For You know my present pains."

The world considers the Lord as the prophet, as Elijah, or as Jeremiah [Matt 16.13-14]. They grossly misunderstand You. "O Lord! How the people misunderstand me . . . O Lord! Henceforth I will never misunderstand You. Whatever You have appointed for me, I will not say, Why, Lord?"

In former days, whenever I received an order from the Lord I considered it too hard, too lonesome for me to fulfill. I even regarded it as an indication that the Lord did not care for me, so He laid such a heavy burden on me. Now I know that all His plans for me are but love. The grace of the Lord Jesus is always sufficient. My past thought of the Lord totally misunderstood Him. "O Lord! From now on, whatever You want me to do and to fulfill, be it suffering or joy, I am willing to accept it from Your loving heart. I dare not misunderstand my beloved Lord anymore. Others may not be satisfied with the Lord; but I am always satisfied with You, and I always love You."

Fat and big fellows deem the road narrow because of their fatness and largeness. Thin and little fellows do not regard the road as narrow because of their thinness and smallness. Jesus spoke of the narrow gate and the straitened way (Matt. 7.13-14). Relatively speaking, so narrow and straitened is this way to the big fellows that they find it hard to walk in it; but to the little fellows they find it easy, for the gate is not so narrow nor the way so straitened to them. The burden of the Lord is light, and His yoke is easy (Matt. 11.30). We should forsake our fat and big "self" to do the Lord's will. "O Lord! I confess to You that when my heart inclines towards self-desire, I judge Your word hard and Your will difficult. But when I wholly seek Your will, I know there is no wider gate and broader way in the whole universe than the will of God." The will of the Lord remains the same. Difficult or easy depends on whether a person inclines to his own will or submits to the Lord's will. May the Lord be my will, and I be nothing.

"O Lord! I know if I go to another place to preach, probably more souls will surrender to You. But, now, because You order me to guard Your border, I dare not move. Here, I am not able to save souls, yet this is Your appointed place for me. I therefore ask You to make me faithful and deliver me from the love of success. Faithful to the thing in hand, faithful to what the Lord has ordained for me. O Lord! Because I love You, I long to see people saved and belong to You. Nevertheless, Your desire is for me to hold the fort. I would rather not save souls that I may please Your heart. O Lord! Your will is the very best. I am willing to obey—to be faithful without seeking for success."

May the Lord take away from me all my earthly friends that I may commune with Him without fluctuation.

"O Lord! Since the world has no love for me and has deserted me, I ask You to protect my loneliness. This solitude in You enables me to have You as my constant companion."

"But thou continuest . . ." (Heb. 1.11-13). O Lord! All are gone; will You go, too? No, "but thou continuest." How undependable are men; You alone are everlasting—lasting ever for me. Thank the Lord!

I sometimes ponder that I have some good but am not loved; I have tribulations but receive no sympathy; I am lonely and poor but am not noticed and cared about. When I die, there will be no one weeping by my coffin. "O Lord! Do I have to end my life this way?"

"O Lord! I really love You. All that concerns You, I

love. I love to hear (hear preaching), I love to read (the Bible), I love to speak (preach), I love to exalt You (praise), I love to converse with You (prayer). I love You because You first loved me."

Let me not be loved by men, because human love may create a misty separation between You and me. I only want Your love, and I love You alone.

You truly are my sufficiency (Gen. 33.9). Having You, I have all things. There will not be any circumstance that I am not happy with.

It is easy to offer to God that which we are able to do. It is hard, however, to offer the heart of offering to God. It is relatively easy to offer up Isaac; but to offer the heart of offering up Isaac, that is, the desire to regain Isaac and let God keep one's heart, that is fairly hard. If this is hard, it proves that we are more concerned with our integrity. We have not died to self. We should not have such a dead-set offering. (The old Chinese proverb says, "Once having mounted, it is hard to dismount.")

"O Lord! I do not desire Your reward; I desire You."

May the Lord help me to maintain a pilgrim's attitude while sojourning on earth. I must never plan to stay here long. I do not know how few are the days I will stay in this day-to-day inn.

It may be today. "I come again, and will receive you unto myself" (John 14.3). What joy!

Having had a picture taken of myself with a few believers, I wrote on the side of the photo: "We know that, if he shall be manifested, we shall be like him" (1 John 3.2). How wonderful!

Many sufferings today for the Lord double future joy.

Today's cross-bearing shall be exchanged for tomorrow's glorious crown. "O Lord! Do You regard me as unworthy to suffer with You? Why is it that no tribulation comes my way this day? Anyway, have Your own will. Do not give me suffering for my sake. Order whatever pleases You."

5. There was a day (in fact, today, 28 December 1923) in which I felt I could not love the Lord. I prayed unceasingly, but I did not sense any love for the Lord. New light came to me. I believe I truly love Him. I praise Him because He loves me. He loves me. He loves me. Wonderful love that loves even me. Now I realize it is not I who love Him; it is He who loves me. Whenever I look within, I see myself and am conscious of how little, if any, I love Him. The more I look at myself, the less I sense my love for Him. But when I look at Him and taste of His love, I am melted in His love. My love for the Lord spontaneously arises. Love the Lord by faith. "O Lord! Although I could not love You, You love me, and so I love You too."

If it were not because of the comfort of the Lord, the affection of the Lord, and the help of the Lord, I would have long been in despair and have died.

"O Lord! Once I entered into Your secret place and was so filled with Your presence. Now I will not be satisfied if my communion with You is but even a few degrees lower than what it was that day."

The Lord's heart is joyful; why should I therefore be anxious? Some say to me: "He who lives by faith uses lots of stamps," which refers to a person using many postal stamps to inform people how he lives by trusting the Lord and how he helps the Lord in His work. This actually is a huge obstacle to faith.

Once a matter is committed to the Lord, it should not be taken back for self-working. The greatest temptation is that after a matter is committed to the Lord, a person reckons that for the Lord to accomplish His work he must spend time to help it be done as though the Lord needs help (see Ps. 37.5). "O Lord! If You desire it for me, You have to bring it to pass. If it is not Your wish, and even though I may be able to work for it, I will not move. Because what I want is Your will."

"O Lord! May the work I do be a self-dying work. Let no one see it except Him whose eye looks from above."

Psalm 88.18: "Lover and friend hast thou put far from me." Some have died, some have departed, some have no knowledge of me. As long as the name of the Lord is praised, what else do I ask for?

"O Lord! Satan and men try to hinder Your work. Will You not intervene while Your little one is placed in such spiritual danger?"

May the love of the Lord be so special to me that I am unable to have my own will on anything.

In former days when I was in trouble, I saw Your faithfulness, and I took You as my bosom friend. Now my sorrow (actually joy) is greatly increased. Worldly friends and Christian associates are all undependable. Misunderstandings many, affections vacillating; but You are different, for You never change. You and I, I and You, are truly joined into one. Now You are really my life. Formerly I could live without You, but now I cannot live for a moment without You.

During December 1923 I was often sick. I felt ashamed in my sickness, for I could not utter the word found in Song of Solomon 5.8, "I am sick from love."

Do not imagine that because you forsake all for the Lord's sake and work for Him, you add glory to Him. Know that the Lord's work is holy work. That He is willing to give His work to you to do is bestowing upon you great grace and honor.

"O Lord! I today desire You yourself more than Your gift as I had done in the past. O Lord! I want You."

"Let others live a peaceful life, having their names on people's lips, all their wishes granted, their influence great, their life full of spiritual power, their work bearing much fruit, and their faith daily increasing; but as for me, I want only the will of God. O Lord, I do not care how You treat others, I only want Your will and want to please You. Your will is the sweetest and the most precious."

Psalm 106.15: "he gave them their request, but sent leanness into their soul." O Lord! I would only ask what the Lord wishes me to ask; do not hear my own prayers.

I now walk faithfully with You step by step till I shall walk into glory.

"O Lord! Not that I crave to serve You more, but that I always long to rejoice Your heart. If Your heart is painful, my tears will flow. What is the use of labor?" (At this point I shed many tears.)

I want to dwell in Your heart, rest on Your breast,

and walk in Your path. Nowhere else could gladden Your heart, and neither could it please me.

"I do not love work, neither do I love not to work. I do not seek for my spiritual progress, nor do I seek for my spiritual regress. O Lord! What is Your mind? If You want me to advance spiritually and work, I will advance and work. All is for You, not for me."

"But I said, I have labored in vain, I have spent my strength for nought and vanity; yet surely the justice due to me is with Jehovah, and my recompense with my God. And now saith Jehovah that formed me from the womb to be his servant, to bring Jacob again to him, and that Israel be gathered unto him (for I am honorable in the eyes of Jehovah, and my God is become my strength)" (Is. 49.4-5). This chapter of the Bible speaks of Christ as servant. But we who are fellow servants with the Lord can imitate Him. The words in verses 4 and 5 move my heart. These words are spoken by the servant of the Lord. Christ was sent to save "the lost sheep of the house of Israel" (Matt. 15.24), but He was rejected by the children of Israel. From the human viewpoint Christ seemed to have accomplished nothing. Jehovah sent Him "to bring Jacob again to him," and yet He could not cause "Israel [to] be gathered unto him." Outwardly He had "labored in vain," and had "spent [his] strength for nought and vanity." Yet, Jesus was "obedient even unto death" (Phil. 2.8). He faithfully did the Father's will and denied His own will (see John 5). So that while on earth Jesus was "honorable in the eyes of Jehovah" and "God is become [his] strength."

We all are God's servants. We seek to be faithful to

the Father's business, notwithstanding its result. Even if one preaches for ten years without a soul saved, the work is counted as gold, silver and costly stones if it is done in faithful obedience to God. If a work is not done for the Lord but for name and profit (holy name and holy profit)—yea, for the glory of men and the enjoyment of self, then such work is reckoned as wood, hay and stubble (cf. 1 Cor. 3.12ff.). Let it be known that if I am faithful and obedient, and though I may not accomplish anything, I have glory in the eyes of the Lord. It is the Lord who judges. It is His work; therefore, let us not seek men's approval but only His pleasure. The Lord is our all, and we seek nothing but the Lord.

All that is good belongs to the Lord; all that is bad belongs to me.

"Even so let your light shine before men; that they may see your good works, and glorify your Father who is in heaven" (Matt. 5.16). The light shines before men not for the purpose of being seen by men but for the reason that they may glorify God. A beautiful life is not lived for the purpose of being a biography to be read but is for the glory of God. Studying God's word is not for the sake of collecting materials for one's preaching but for the advancement of one's spiritual life. Even the progress in spiritual life is not for the purpose of giving a person more joy but for giving pleasure to the Lord's heart.

"O Lord! I will soon go to the country place to restore my soul. You know my present distress. According to human eyes, my physical weakness has increased, though I am still healthy in You. O Lord! My beloved Lord! Arise and work, or else I will probably go to You before Your return. May the Lord's will be done!"

6. "How dare I withhold anything which may please Your heart? How dare I not surrender absolutely for Your will to be done? O Lord! Please go ahead and work. Your servant quietly waits for Your sending."

"At any time, to any place, for any person, O Lord! May Your will be done."

"Ye put to shame the counsel of the poor, because Jehovah is his refuge" (Ps. 14.6). "Because" in the margin is "but"—"O Lord! What can I say, for having You is all-sufficient for me."

"Without You I do not know how to live. From my youth till now, I always longed to have a friend. Now I have had You!"

"A disciple is not above his teacher, nor a servant above his lord" (see Matt. 10.24-25). Do not ever imagine to have no suffering in this world. Whenever suffering comes, ask the question—How is this suffering to be compared with the Lord's?

"No one knoweth the Son, save the Father" (Matt. 11.27). O Lord! How lonely You were! You were satisfied with doing the Father's will. How can I be discontented since I have You who know me?

We often think about how we can repay the Lord; we therefore rarely praise Him. The more we realize how *impossible* it is for us to reimburse Him, the more we will have the heart and voice of praise, for that is all we can do.

A grain of wheat is beautiful to look at, but it remains a single grain. For this reason, I must not accept the praise of men as though I am able. Like that grain of wheat, let me fall into the ground and die. Let me be hidden in death and be unknown to men. Thus will I, like the fallen grain, bear much fruit. After death, the fruit belongs to the owner of the garden. The dead grain has disappeared. May all glory be to God.

During these months, each time I have taken up my pen to write these "Musings under the Cross," I have written with tears. Now, though, these musings should be concluded. The Lord is coming soon. The sufferings are either passed or will soon be passed. The battle is won, and the victory song is heard. Indeed, this may be the final mile to travel! Very soon I shall meet the Lord and be with Him forever. My feet will not ache anymore.

May our hearts ascend to the heights we have never reached before. May the love of Christ so constrain us that the most beautiful, most admirable, and most glorious things and events and people of this world turn, by comparison, to be detestable. May our blessed hope so fill us that the persecutions, sufferings, misunderstandings and trials of the world become something to be welcomed by us: because they enhance our spiritual progress and set our mind on Jesus. His smiling face and His satisfaction enable us willingly to tread the thorny path. How much easier is this path of ours than the one which He had traveled! May God preserve us through this despicable, dark scene till at last Jesus—our Morning Star—appears (Rev. 22.16).

3 | A Pilgrim Song*

Behind is the deserted world,

Before lies my ultimate goal,

Speed on the appointed course,

Bearing the cross.

No looking back! No lingering on!

Home is near.

The Lord's love is inexhaustible;

A few more miles,

Comes the rest;

No heartbreak, no tears, no weariness!

---

*This was composed on 28 May 1924, and subsequently that same year appeared in *Spiritual Light* magazine.—*Translator*

4 | Still Unknown*

After all, I have not yet seen You—that kind face, the nail-pierced hands and feet, the thorn-crowned brow, the spear-pierced side, and those weeping eyes of Yours mourning for my sins. Fortunately I have first tasted Your sweet love and am thus comforted somewhat.

After all, I have not yet seen You. How I long to fly at once to You and pour forth . . . Let your hands embrace me to Your breast; let them touch my head. Oh, that I may see and love the One whom I have not seen, yet loved for many years. How I often pray for Your speedy return that I may earlier see You . . .

I frequently think: As soon as I see Your face, I will mention the longings I had for You while I was on earth. The tears I shed in sufferings and trials You will wipe away drop by drop. How You will comfort me.

---

*This writing appeared in *Spiritual Light* magazine for 23 September 1924.—*Translator.*

What a time of exuberant joy! Yet, I suppose that of the many words I have planned to say to You not one of them shall easily escape my mouth—because joy has so filled my heart. All these ten thousand words are summed up in but one word—"I love You."

Why is it that You do not come immediately? O Lord, come quickly!

I sigh and I labor in this earthly tabernacle. What distresses me most is that since I cannot go, why do You not come?

Yet, O Lord, if You should come that day, what would be the end of the people of the world? As for myself, how very few are the fruits I bear. If you were to come now, how could I possibly gain the pleasure of bearing the cross daily? How would I ever learn obedience through suffering? How could I have the experience of being lonely for Your sake? How could I experience the blessing of being yoked together with You? How would I ever know the delicate way You had wished to deal with me? How would I finally realize the insufficiency of my love for You? How would I at last know the selfishness of my love for You?

But because You delay Your coming, You now lead me through the fire. You cause me to pass through water. In this narrow path, I walk with You along a way few people ever travel. If You should therefore come that day, how poor and blind I must appear before You, so unprepared am I.

However, my warm desire for Your coming is not diminished. For what can satisfy my heart is You. Though You are far away, I long for You. The thought of Your coming gives me full satisfaction; Your delay increases my bodily wounds. Let the old pass and the new come. Let my mouth utter unceasingly the sound of praise, and let my spirit always touch Your nearness.

Your time for coming is never too late. What You see fit is the best. I only know that all things work together for good, since nothing comes to me without passing through Your hand.

O Lord, when is the best day, after all? Can your coming be today? Oh, Lord, how about today? When You come, may You find me in Your preordained way.

5 | Help in the Spirit*

I sense very deeply that all subjects dealt with in writing or in speaking must be handled under the direction of the Lord. Only thus will they help people's spirit. What teaching we receive from the Lord naturally profits our spirit at that moment. Then it seems to be stored in our mind. If we teach out of the memory of our mind, those who receive our teaching will only have a momentary impression left in their mind. In our spirit God should renew the teaching which we are familiar with before we deliver it to the people. Then life will flow into their spirit. This is power. This is life.

"The words that I have spoken unto you," said Jesus, "are spirit, and are life" (John 6.63). And why? Because what He says is commanded by God instead of it being spoken out from himself. The Lord often reminds me that only what comes from the spirit begets spirit. Nothing less could profit the spirit.

---

*This appeared in *Spiritual Light* magazine (1924?). —*Translator*

PART TWO

THE WORD OF THE CROSS*

*Part Two consists of six chapters on this general theme. The author completed writing the contents of chapters 1 to 5 on 26 April 1924 at Jade Forest Hall Cottage in Foochow, southern China. They subsequently appeared in *Spiritual Light* magazine (1924?). The contents of Chapter 6, however, first appeared separately, and later, in another Chinese-language magazine.—*Translator*

1 | The Word of the Cross

How commendable it is that in spite of the profusion in recent days of heresies and apostasies trying to wipe out "the word of the cross," there is still a group of zealous believers who hold fast to the cross and propagate the salvation of the cross. Yet what I find in print as well as in the pulpit concerning the word of the cross does not seem to be systematic, and is sometimes over-simplified, thus unable to benefit those young believers very much. Hence, I would write down here that which the Lord has shown me, so that His name may be glorified and His word may prevail. Amen.

"The word of the cross" has neither beginning nor end. It cannot be measured by time. For the Lamb has been slain from the foundation of the world (Rev. 13.8 mg.). The life of a Christian originates from the cross and is perfected by the cross. If a believer is real, he must trust in the cross. The word of the cross and the believer's life are inseparable.

The cross is composed of two sides: and these are inseparable. On the one side of the cross is death; on the other side is resurrection. In the natural realm there is a great gap between man's death and life; but in the spiritual realm, death and life are indivisible. "Death" deals with sin, while "life" deals with righteousness. A natural man is not able to know death since he does not even know life. Yet how can the spiritual man know life if he does not know death? Please take note of these two sides of the cross: "death," and "life."

I. The Death Side of the Cross

On the death side, there are again two aspects—namely, "substitution," and "identification" or "co-death." These two aspects gather up all the significance of the words, "the death of the cross."

A. *Substitution.* This aspect speaks of Christ having died for us. He died for sinners. He stood in the place of sinners. Almost all the types in the Old Testament concerning the suffering of the Lord Jesus refer to this aspect. The offering of sacrifices points to the substitutionary death of the Lord Jesus. Nowhere is this more distinctive than in Isaiah 53 where the substitution of the Lord Jesus is mentioned twelve times:

1. "Surely he hath borne our griefs" (v.4).
2. "And carried our sorrows" (v.4).
3. "He was wounded for our transgressions" (v.5).
4. "He was bruised for our iniquities" (v.5).

5. "The chastisement of our peace was upon him" (v.5).
6. "With his stripes we are healed" (v.5).
7. "Jehovah hath laid on him the iniquity of us all" (v.6).
8. "He was cut off out of the land of the living for the transgression of my people" (v.8).
9. "Thou shalt make his soul an offering for sin" (v.10).
10. "He shall bear their iniquities" (v.11).
11. "He [bore] the sin of many" (v.12).
12. "And made intercession for the transgressors" (v.12).

In the New Testament the concept of "substitution" is made even clearer. For the lost, the Lord Jesus came "to give his life a ransom for many" (Matt. 20.28). To shepherd us, He "lay down [his] life for the sheep" (John 10.15). As to the Church, He "purchased [it] with his own blood" (Acts 20.28). "While we were yet weak, in due season Christ died for the ungodly. . . . While we were yet sinners, Christ died for us" (Rom. 5.6,8). The first stage of the "gospel" is that "Christ died for our sins according to the scriptures" (1 Cor. 15.3). For He is God and He is man, and therefore He "died for all" (2 Cor. 5.14). Because we have sinned, Christ "who knew no sin he [God] made to be sin on our behalf" (2 Cor. 5.21). "Though he [Christ] was rich, yet for your sakes he became poor" (2 Cor. 8.9). Had we not sinned and been poor, we would not need His death. Unfortunately, we have all sinned; hence the Lord Jesus could not but become sin for us. He died as our substitute on the cross, bearing the penalty of sin.

Christ "having become a curse for us," the result was that He "redeemed us from the curse of the law" and the method was that He "hang[ed] on a tree" (Gal. 3.13). And now "we have our redemption through his blood, the forgiveness of our trespasses" (Eph. 1.7). "Who his own self [and no other] bare our sins [and not his own] in his body upon the tree" (1 Peter 2.24). "Because Christ also suffered for sins once, the righteous for the unrighteous" (1 Peter 3.18). The substitutionary work of Christ is now finished. All who believe in Him shall not perish but have eternal life.

In this aspect of substitution four distinguishing facts are included; namely, (1) that all are sinners; (2) that the wages of sin is death; (3) that the Lord Jesus died for all; and (4) that whosoever believes—that is, receives—the Lord Jesus as Savior, is exempt from perdition and possesses eternal life. If one's knowledge of the word of the cross has not reached this stage, he is not yet saved. Indeed, what follows below will not profit anyone like that. So that unless a person has first come to the cross and accepted the Lord Jesus who was lifted up as his Savior, he is not able to advance to the next stage of the word of the cross.

B. *Identification or Co-Death.* Believing in the substitutionary death of Jesus saves us from the penalty of sin. Co-death with Christ delivers us from the power of sin. For in His death on the cross Christ Jesus not only died for sinners but also took sinners with Him to die. He not only died for sin, He also died to sin: not merely bore the penalty of sin, but also destroyed the power of sin. He caused sinners to die to sin as well as to be freed from the recompense of sin: "knowing this, that our old man was crucified with him [the Lord Jesus]" (Rom. 6.6). The word "crucified" in the Greek is a "living" word, for it varies in tense according to the time indicated. Here, it is the aorist tense; that is, it is so used when the moral import is an abiding one, and when time is not in question (see the Bible translation of J. Nelson Darby, his note "k" on Romans 6.6). It is therefore a once and forever form, which means—once done, forever done. Our "old I" has been crucified with the Lord Jesus: it is an eternally completed fact.

In reading the entire Bible we cannot find a single command saying, "Crucify your old man." This is because our co-death with Christ is an accomplished fact. Just as Christ died for sin once and dies no more, so we who once died with Him on the cross need not to be crucified again today. In order to experience this co-death in our life we need only to believe in this fact related to us in Romans 6.6, and not try to exert our strength to put the old man to death. Just as you are saved by believing in the substitutionary death of the Lord Jesus, so you are delivered from sin and have the body of sin done away with by believing your old man was crucified with Him. The reality of "co-death" and "substitutionary death" is all obtained through faith.

"Identification" or "co-death" has also two different aspects: (1) upon once believing that the old man has been crucified, there must be a daily living in this co-death with Christ; and (2) there must be a taking up of the cross daily. The first aspect has to do with a perfect fact. Once a believer accepts this fact, he daily maintains this death even amid seeming appearances that the old man is not dead. Thus shall sin have no power over him. The second aspect is somewhat different. It is a daily experience of the cross: for the Lord's sake, the believer will daily forsake his legitimate rights in this world. This thus differs from the first aspect of forsaking sin.

"Substitutionary death" naturally leads to "co-death." "One died for all" and the result was that "therefore all died" (2 Cor. 5.14). The Lord Jesus died for me and I died in the Lord Jesus. Romans 6 develops on this further: (a) "we who died to sin" (v.2); (b) "baptized into his death" (v.3); (c) "through baptism into death" (v.4); and, (d) "united with him in the likeness of his death" (v.5). All these expand on the meaning of "co-death."

This "death" includes various attitudes of the believer: (1) with respect to sin, the Bible says, "Reckon ye also yourselves to be dead unto sin" (Rom. 6.11); (2) with respect to the "old I," the Bible says that "our old man was crucified with him, that the body of sin might be done away" (Rom. 6.6); (3) with respect to the law, God's word indicates that with the law comes the knowledge of sin (see Rom 7.7). Sin and the law are closely related. "Ye also were made dead to the law" (Rom. 7.4); (4) with respect to the flesh, the Scriptures say: "they that are of Christ Jesus have crucified the flesh with the passions and the lusts thereof" (Gal. 5.24); (5) with respect to the world, the Scriptures indicate that "through [the cross] the world hath been crucified unto me, and I unto the world" (Gal.

6.14); and (6) with respect to the present age, the Bible tells us that if "ye died with Christ from the rudiments of the world, why [are ye] as though living in the world . . .?" (Col. 2.20) The above six points refer to the attitudes which those who have died with Christ must daily maintain.

What the Lord Jesus said about denying self daily and taking up the cross to follow Him points especially to "suffering" and "shame." For to Him the cross is also shame; indeed, our Lord despised its shame (see Heb. 12.2), but so shall we despise shame too. In Philippians 3.10 Paul noted the same thing: "that I may know . . . the fellowship of his sufferings, becoming conformable unto his death."

This kind of co-death is quite different from the six points mentioned before. For this has to do with forfeiting legitimate rights, just as in the example of Christ who "poured out his soul unto death" (Is. 53.12). "Soul" here comprises man's intellect, feeling and affection. All these are legitimate. Yet our Lord "poured out his soul unto death." In a similar vein Paul said, "I die daily" (1 Cor. 15.31).

This stage of life runs parallel to the lesson to be learned in the "life" aspect of the cross (see that discussion below): "we who live are always delivered unto death for Jesus' sake, that the life also of Jesus may be manifested in our mortal flesh" (2 Cor. 4.11). Before we proceed to the "life" side we should daily be delivered unto death for the Lord's sake: die to our environment, die to the world's praise and slander, die to fleshly works, die to words, and die to opinions. Then the life of the Lord Jesus will be manifested and much fruit will be produced (see John 12.24).

"Death" is the believer's passive way with sin, whereas "life" is his active way with righteousness. Without passing through death, life will not come. Passing through death does not require years; it is an act of faith. The moment a person believes in the substitutionary death of the Lord Jesus, at that very moment he believes he receives new life. Many believers are stuck in the "death" position, and thus they are very weak and without power. In their death they fail to experience life. Such believers need also to believe in their life in the Lord Jesus so that they may have the strength to grow.

II. The Life Side of the Cross

The "life" side comprises three aspects; which are, (1) alive with the Lord; (2) the Lord lives in me; and (3) live for the Lord. Upon completing these three aspects, the believer shall live a victorious life. Before proceeding further, however, I must say something so that there will be no misunderstanding. I do not mean that only after people come to the life side do they have life, for when a person believes in the substitutionary death of the Lord Jesus he is born from above with a new life. Through the working together of this new life and the Holy Spirit he is able to believe that the old man was crucified, thus opening the way to the life side. Gradually he advances in the Lord till he attains maturity. We are first made alive together with

Christ before we are raised up with Him (see Eph. 2.5-6).

A. *Alive with the Lord.* In the natural realm, the law of living beings is life before death. But in the spiritual realm it is the reverse; that is to say, death precedes life: "We were buried therefore with him through baptism into death: that like as Christ was raised from the dead through the glory of the Father, so we also might walk in newness of life" (Rom. 6.4). The death of Christ is not a lasting death, since His soul was not left in Hades nor did his body see corruption (see Ps. 16.10); He has risen. Therefore, "if we have become united with him in the likeness of his death, we shall be also in the likeness of his resurrection" (Rom. 6.5).

Although you have not yet tasted the fullness of this new life, you should know that this is God's pronouncement which you must truly believe. You so reckon yourself as dead to sin and "alive unto God in Christ Jesus" (Rom. 6.11). If you have reckoned yourself dead to sin, you should also reckon yourself as alive unto God. As the power of God made Christ live, so the same power makes us live with Christ (see 2 Cor. 13.4). This is a fixed rule: "having been buried with him in baptism, wherein ye were also raised with him through faith in the working of God, who raised him from the dead" (Col. 2.12). Therefore, being raised with the Lord Jesus from the dead is God's fact. It is now only a matter of whether you believe or not. By believing, Christ is already in you.

B. *The Lord lives in me:* "always bearing about in the body the dying of Jesus, that the life also of Jesus may be manifested in our body" (2 Cor. 4.10). What is mentioned in A. above is God's fact. Paul believed it, hence here it became his personal spiritual experience. The life of the Lord Jesus Christ dwelt in him and was also manifested through him: "I have been crucified with Christ; and it is no longer I that live, but Christ liveth in me" (Gal. 2.20). Here Paul clearly reckoned as fact that "Christ lives in [him]." Since Christ was his life, he was now filled with Christ as he once was filled with the "old man." Naturally he lived as Christ had lived. This makes a real "Christian."

C. *Live for the Lord.* The length and width and height and depth of the love of Christ is incomprehensible. But with the aforesaid experience one should be able to live for Christ. To live for the Lord is being touched by His love. To live for the Lord is the aftermath of believing in the Lord who laid down His life for all. So Paul continued to declare the following in Galatians 2.20: "that life which I now live in the flesh I live in faith, the faith which is in the Son of God, who loved me, and gave himself up for me." We who are alive in the Lord are so constrained by the immense love of Christ in dying on the cross for us that we will live for Him: "he died for all, that they that live [for through Him believers have been made alive] should no longer live unto themselves, but unto him who for their sakes died and rose again" (2 Cor. 5.15). Whether we live or die, we are the Lord's. Having received the love of Christ, we should declare with Paul: "to me to live is Christ, and to die is gain" (Phil. 1.21).

In reaching this stage in spiritual experience a Christian's life becomes victorious. If one dies daily he lives daily: if one dies to sin he is alive unto the Lord. And he thereby advances to a life of spiritual warfare with Satan. Most Christians today know only the conflict in Romans 7. Who knows that this is but battling with the old man, and therefore such cannot be called spiritual warfare. Spiritual warfare is a wrestling with forces in the spiritual realm, even against Satan and his wicked spirits. Having died and been raised, one's life is hid with Christ in God (see Col. 3.1-3). This is ascension life.

In the Letter to the Ephesians we are told that our life is one of being seated with Christ in the heavenly places (Eph. 2.6), and in chapter 1 it reads, "and made him [the Lord Jesus] to sit at his [the Father's] right hand in the heavenly places, far above all rule, and authority, and power, and dominion [that of Satan and his servants], and every name that is named, not only in this world, but also in that which is to come" (Eph. 1.20-21). Hence our life is now in the heavenly places, and Satan is trodden under our feet. The cross alone gives such victory: "having despoiled the principalities and the powers, he made a show of them openly, triumphing over them in it [the cross]" (Col. 2.15); and, "they overcame him [Satan the accuser] because of the blood of the Lamb" (Rev. 12.11). Hallelujah! Christ is Victor. By His cross we too can overcome Satan and accomplish the Lord's work. Hallelujah!

To help the reader understand, a diagram is given below:

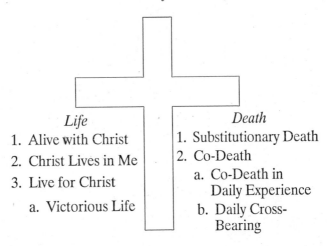

Life
1. Alive with Christ
2. Christ Lives in Me
3. Live for Christ
   a. Victorious Life

Death
1. Substitutionary Death
2. Co-Death
   a. Co-Death in Daily Experience
   b. Daily Cross-Bearing

This diagram is drawn according to an understanding of the believer's gradual advance in the word of the cross. It seems to us to be correct according to the light of the Bible. May the reader believe and obey the Christ of the cross. Amen.

2 | How Christ Died for Us

The Scriptures have a number of ways to explain the substitutionary death of the Lord Jesus. Each way has its special emphasis, though all speak of the substitutionary death. Thus its hidden meanings are fully developed. May the Spirit of God reveal to us the mystery of the substitutionary death. Amen.

1. *Became Sin*: "Him who knew no sin he [God] made to be sin on our behalf" (2 Cor. 5.21). We all know the holiness, goodness and purity of Christ. This goes without need of saying much. This verse indicates that we are not only sinners but we all have sinned. It also suggests that the Lord Jesus became sin in order to take away the sin of the world (see John 1.29). The cross of Calvary exposes the climax of sin. Unless He had become sin for us, the Lord Jesus could not have suffered the penalty of sin for us. How immense is the grace of the Lord that He who fiercely hated sin became sin for us.

2. *Gives Life*: ". . . to give his life a ransom for

many" (Matt. 20.28). The very word "ransom" indicates that the "many" had sold themselves. Without their being sold, there would not be the need for them to be redeemed. When our forefathers sinned, they did so deliberately. Since mankind was sold to sin (the natural man is the devil's possession, so he is called the devil's child—see John 8.44), and because God is righteous, He could not take mankind back by force. God therefore used the life of Jesus to be our ransom money to redeem us back to himself: the life of the perfect Son of God given for the lives of sinners. The price of sinners is almost equal to the price of the Son of God. How great is God's love towards men! (Let us note that in His substitutionary death the Lord Jesus obeyed God and laid down His life voluntarily; see John 10.17-18).

3. *Died for Sins*: "Christ died for our sins according to the scriptures" (1 Cor. 15.3). The Lord Jesus having been made sin and having died for sin, His death is not in vain. Since the Lord Jesus became sin for us, He must also have died for our sins, for the wages of sin is death. The word "our" here in 1 Corinthians 15 indicates that He did not die for His own sin (for He knew no sin). Though Jesus for our sake—and not for His own self—became sin, He did not die for His own self but died for our sins. For this reason, we who believe in Jesus shall not die for our sins, since He has already borne the consequences of all sins: "Christ also suffered for sins once" (1 Peter 3.18).

4. *Died for Us*: "while we were yet sinners, Christ died for us" (Rom. 5.8). We are sinners. Let us note that according to the Biblical definition the word "sin-

ner" does not only imply that the one who sins is a sinner. To be more accurate, it denotes that all men and women are sinners, and that all also sin. Thus we are sinning sinners. The wages of sin is death, and the "soul that sinneth, it shall die" (Eze. 18.4). In Romans 5 we all are labeled as (1) weak (v.6); (2) ungodly (v.6); (3) sinners (v.8); and (4) enemies (v.10). This is because we descend from the first man Adam, and so we are weak, ungodly, sinners, and enemies. Hence, we must bear the consequence of this fourfold phenomena, which is "death." But Christ having died for us, we naturally are set free. (In Point 2 above, Gives Life, the emphasis is on *the Lord*; here the emphasis is on *for us*). He not only died for us—for His sheep (John 10.15), He also died for the Church (Eph. 5.25), even for all (2 Cor. 5.14)—that is to say, for the whole world (1 John 2.2). Unfortunately the world does not believe in Him, so it forfeits salvation.

5. *Upon the Cross.* People love to talk about the Lord Jesus and His death, but they dislike talking about the Lord Jesus and the cross. Even today the cross is an offense to many. But what Paul preached was Jesus Christ and Him crucified (1 Cor. 2.2). And Peter wrote: "who his own self bare our sins in his body upon the tree" (1 Peter 2.24). Moses in Deuteronomy and Paul in Galatians develop this point still further: "he that is hanged [on a tree] is accursed of God" (Deut. 21.23); and, "Christ redeemed us from the curse of the law, having become a curse for us; for it is written, Cursed is every one that hangeth on a tree" (Gal. 3.13). Thus the death of the Lord Jesus is not an ordinary one. It is the meanest and most

shameful of deaths. Without His awful death, we could not be delivered from the curse of the law. Once Christ died upon the cross, however, salvation triumphed; for Jesus cried out from the cross: "It is finished" (John 19.30).

6. *Gave Himself*: "He saved others; himself he cannot save. . . . Let him now come down from the cross" (Matt. 27.42). These are the words spoken by the Jews at that time. They mocked our Lord as being able to save others but unable to save himself. They did not know that even then the Lord could have saved himself by calling for the aid of twelve legions of angels. Yet for the sake of doing the Father's will and saving the world, Christ would not come down from the cross. For the issue was clear: to save himself He must forsake men, but to save men He must forsake himself. How Jesus loved us and gave himself up for us (see Eph. 5.25-27). He gave himself up and gained us. He delivered us out of the present evil world (Gal. 1.4) and redeemed us from all iniquities (Titus 2.14).

7. *Suffered*: "Christ also suffered for sins once, the righteous for the unrighteous" (1 Peter 3.18). The consequence of sin is suffering as well as death. Suffering is prolonged death. In the work of substitutionary death, the Lord Jesus suffered from the people of that period for thirty-three years. Then at Calvary, He further suffered—for men's sins as well as for sin itself. And He suffered the pains of death for six hours. He took away the suffering of sin so that we could have the "joy of salvation" (Ps. 51.21).

8. *Offered Up Himself*: "it is impossible that the blood of bulls and goats should take away sins" (Heb.

10.4). Men sin, therefore there needs to be man who comes to redeem. "It is the blood that maketh atonement by the reason of the life" (Lev. 17.11). For this cause, Christ came to the world to be man that he might offer himself as a sacrifice and shed His blood to redeem sinners. "He is the propitiation for our sins" (1 John 2.2). The blood of bulls and goats annually offered could merely *cover* men's transgressions; it could not take them away. "For this [atonement] he did once for all, when he offered up himself" (Heb. 7.27). "So Christ also, having been once offered to bear the sins of many . . ." (Heb. 9.28). The original intent which lay behind the offering of the Old Testament sacrifices was that the sacrifice offered would die as a substitute for the sinner. In this respect, then, how perfectly the substitutionary death of Christ has fulfilled that intent.

9. *Tasted Death*. The sting of death is sin (1 Cor. 15.56). The Lord Jesus died for our sins. His death is caused by the poison released by the sting of death. As the Bible makes clear, Jesus tasted death for every man as well as He died for all: "that by the grace of God he should taste of death for every man" (Heb.2.9). In coming to the world the Lord Jesus took upon himself flesh and blood, hence He was able to die: "that through death he [Jesus] might bring to nought . . . and might deliver all . . ." (Heb. 2.14,15). He died for us that we might not die spiritually. He tasted death that we might not die physically.

Hence, this is why the Bible views the believer's death as sleep. Normally after a person dies, his soul enters Hades. The gates of Hades are tightly shut so that the dead cannot get out but will taste of death.

But after the Lord Jesus tasted death for men and was raised from the dead, He broke the gates of Hades. One day we who believe in the Lord Jesus will be awakened from sleep and receive a glorious body. We now are not in fear of death.

10. *Lifted Up*. God dwells in the heavens above, and men live on the earth below. Because of sin, there appears to be a separation between heaven and earth. In His being lifted up, however, the Lord Jesus joins together the true God in heaven and the men on earth. The place of lifting up is between heaven and earth. With respect to heaven the Lord Jesus received the judgment of God; with respect to the earth He bore the iniquity of men. With God's wrath above and sinners below, the Lord Jesus stood in the middle. The wrath of God therefore came upon the Lord Jesus and not upon us. "As Moses lifted up the serpent in the wilderness, even so must the Son of man be lifted up; that whosoever believeth may in him have eternal life" (John 3.14-15). Here Moses symbolizes the law; the serpent, Christ. Men violated the law which came from God. In order to fulfill the law, God could not but lift up Christ on the cross. Such is the action taken by God.

"When ye have lifted up the Son of man . . ." (John 8.28). The word "ye" here in John 8 is referring to "the bondservant[s] of sin" (v.34)—that is, the children of the devil (v.44). All were sinners, bondservants of sin and therefore children of the devil. So God punished the sinful "ye." Christ came to die for the sins of that "ye"; yet He was also lifted up by that same sinful "ye." This explains the human earthly side.

"And I," said Jesus, "if I be lifted up from the earth

. . ." (John 12.32). From this we see that His place is higher than the earth. This indicates that the Lord Jesus is the representative as well as the leader of a new human race. Also, "lifted up from the earth" intimates a place nearer to heaven—to God. From God's viewpoint, He saw only Christ; which means God accepted the substitutionary death of Christ Jesus. "Be lifted up . . . signifying . . . die" (John 12.32-33).

In conclusion, then, the substitutionary death of Christ is seen to be all-inclusive. Formerly we were sinners and deserved eternal perdition. We were without Christ, without God, without hope, without joy. We were destined for sufferings and fear throughout eternity. Happily, Jesus became sin for us and died on the cross as our substitute. We now believe in Him and are eternally saved.

"Hereby know we love, because he laid down his life for us" (1 John 3.16). "Scarcely for a righteous man will one die; for peradventure for the good man some one would even dare to die. But God commendeth his own love toward us, in that, while we were yet sinners, Christ died for us" (Rom. 5.7-8).

3 | Righteousness and Love

The Bible makes two seemingly irreconcilable statements about God and His nature: "He is . . . righteous" (1 John 1.9), and He "is love" (1 John 4.8). "Righteous" deals with the law. There is neither mercy nor love. Whoever violates the law must be punished according to the law. "Love," on the other hand, is kind and merciful. It shows unlimited and irresistible affection towards all, regardless the magnitude of sin. It does not wish that any should suffer; therefore, it is always ready to help and to give joy.

Thus "righteous" and "love" are two opposite natures which ordinarily cannot be reconciled. To be righteous means not to love; and to love means not to be righteous. How wonderful that God has both these natures. How truly great is His grace.

"Jehovah is righteous in all his ways, and gracious in all his works" (Ps. 145.17). This shows how righteousness and love run together.

Being the federal head and representative of mankind, Adam in his sinning represented the sinning of the whole world, both ancient and modern. He thus led all mankind into sin. According to the law of God the wages of sin is death (Rom. 6.23). The soul that sins must die (Eze. 18.4). Adam died on the day he ate, against God's command, the forbidden fruit (Gen. 2.17). Since in Adam all have become sinners, God being righteous must execute the prescribed penalty of the law—death. (While in the flesh, one's spirit is separated from God; this is soon followed by physical death. After the millennium there will be the second death, wherein the resurrected unbelieving man will suffer eternally in the lake of fire.)

Yet God is also love: "For God so loved the world [the sinning sinners]" (John 3.16). How compassionate He is towards the fate of sinful man destined to enter into eternal death, separated from God's face, suffering the burning of eternal fire and the biting of undying worms. Eternally lost, without any remedy. Ages of ages, billions of years, are as nothing in eternity. How can God's heart not be moved by such a situation! He would therefore wish to lift men out of *this* destiny and set them free. He would wish to spare them eternal suffering and instead give them eternal joy.

God is thus both righteous and gracious. On the one hand, if He should punish the world according to law to fulfill righteousness, what could He do for pitiful mankind? This would not speak well of His love. On the other hand, if He should lift the world by forgiving their sins and granting them unlimited blessing, He would reduce His law to emptiness and meaninglessness, and thus His righteousness would be totally wiped out. This His righteous nature cannot tolerate. A seeming dilemma is thus created. It would seem He can neither punish nor forgive. How, then, can both righteousness and love be preserved? For from man's standpoint, righteousness and love cannot be preserved.

Here we see the wonder of God's grace of redemption. On the one hand, being righteous, God had to condemn the sin of the world and execute lawful punishment. But on the other hand, He so loved the world that He sent His only begotten Son the Lord Jesus, who came into the world and was crucified for the sin of the world so that all who believe in Him should not perish but have eternal life. Being righteous, God executes the law; being love, He sent His Son Jesus to receive upon himself the lawful judgment and to die as a substitute. Hereafter, whosoever believes and obeys shall be saved. Thus righteousness is maintained and love given. Hallelujah! Christ died for me!

The substitutionary death of Jesus is now an accomplished fact. To believe in Him is all that is required. Let us note that it is a serious error to think that because the Lord Jesus is the propitiation for the whole world (1 John 2.2), all, then—and regardless whether believing or not—shall have eternal life. For the Bible plainly declares that he who believes has eternal life but he who does not believe is already condemned. For example, in John 3.18 we read: "He that believeth on him [Christ] is not judged; he that believeth not hath been judged already, because he hath not believed on the name of the only begotten Son of God." How could the judged ones have eternal life?

Among other things, to "believe" means to "draw from a bank." God's salvation can be likened to a huge sum of money deposited in a bank. The Bible which is "the word of God," can be taken as a check. All who believe God's word and who draw on salvation, that is to say, accept Jesus as Savior, shall be saved. A pauper first believes that the check is cashable in the bank, and then he goes to the bank to draw it out. And thus has he the fund by which to live.

Calvary's cross joins in one God's righteousness and God's love. The plan which God had planned from the foundation of the world is now declared successful. The Lord Jesus as a substitute has borne the suffering of sinners and set them free. God's righteousness and love are thus fully upheld and realized in the redemption of the Lord Jesus.

It needs to be noted that preachers frequently liken God to a rich man, men to debtors, and the Lord Jesus to a mediator. But they need to take care lest they show forth only the righteousness of God and fail to illustrate His love. The fact of the matter is that salvation is completed through the working together of the love of the Holy Father (whose compassionate heart is love), the grace of the Holy Son (love expressed in grace), and the communion of the Holy Spirit (the communication of that grace to us by the Holy Spirit).

"The ordinances of Jehovah are true, and righteous altogether" (Ps. 19.9). "Herein is love . . . that he [God] . . . sent his Son to be the propitiation for our sins" (1 John 4.10).

4 | The Outcome of Substitutionary Death

The substitutionary death of the Lord Jesus on the cross produces many fruits. Here we shall mention only a few of them.

1. *Regeneration.* Many authors misunderstand this matter of regeneration. They frequently consider it as the totality of spiritual life. They regard regeneration as being "begotten of God" as spoken of in 1 John, together with co-death and co-resurrection with the Lord as found in the epistles. Some quote Colossians 3.3, "your life is hid with Christ in God," in their explanation of regeneration. Though they have not committed any grave error by doing so, they have certainly confused the teaching. Regeneration is but the first stage of spiritual life. When one is regenerated he receives life, though this life is yet to be matured. Co-death and co-resurrection with the Lord is to be experienced after one is regenerated.

Some may have been born again, and yet even by the time of their death they had still not experienced co-death and co-resurrection with Christ. According to the plain teaching of the Scriptures, regeneration deals with the substitutionary death of the cross. It is the initial step towards life. (Please note that all the good works done by the "begotten of God" are works performed *after* regeneration in order to demonstrate regeneration; they are not works done to effect regeneration.) The teaching on regeneration is clearly stated in John 3.16. We know it is the work of the Holy Spirit: "except one be born of water and the Spirit" (v.5). The water here refers to the water of baptism. In actuality, one is born of the Holy Spirit, not of water. Hence, in verse 6 it only says, "born of the Spirit" and not, as in the preceding verse, "born of water and the Spirit."

How does the Holy Spirit accomplish this work? All depends on the substitutionary death of the Lord Jesus. Please read John 3.5-15. Verses 5 and 6 speak of regeneration as the work of the Holy Spirit. Verse 14 intimates the substitutionary death of the Lord Jesus in His being lifted up on the cross, just as Moses in his day lifted up the brazen serpent in the wilderness; so that all who believe have eternal life. Hence, in regeneration the Holy Spirit applies the substitutionary death of the cross to the sinner; and as the sinner believes, He puts life into the forgiven one.

Without the cross there is no possibility of regeneration. The cross and regeneration are inseparable. In these verses from John 3, "must" is used twice: one is in verse 7, "Ye must be born anew," and the other is in verse 14, "even so must the Son of man be lifted up." These two "musts" are intimately related. As the Lord Jesus must die to save sinners, so sinners must receive revelation concerning the finished work of the cross by the Holy Spirit. The moment one believes, he is born anew; and in being regenerated he receives life. Though this life is yet to be matured, it nonetheless is sufficient to last eternally. Hence it is called eternal life (v.15).

2. *Forgiveness of sins*. "Sins forgiven" bespeaks God's negative dealing with sinners. We committed the darkest, the dirtiest and most hideous sins. We regard ourselves as unpardonable. Yet because of the substitutionary death of the Lord Jesus, we are being forgiven: "in whom [i.e., in the beloved Son] we have our redemption through his blood, the forgiveness of our trespasses" (Eph. 1.7, see also Col. 1.14). According to God's law, "apart from the shedding of blood there is no remission" (Heb. 9.22). Having the Lord Jesus die and shed His blood for us, God surely will forgive our sins.

3. *Justification*. As we have seen, "forgiveness" is God's negative way with sinners; whereas "justification" bespeaks God's positive grace towards sinners. To "forgive" shows that men have sinned but they are forgiven. To "justify" declares that men have been acquitted as though without sin and are therefore justified. In a court of law the guilty person is sometimes forgiven and the righteous person is pronounced not guilty. Christ died for us, therefore we are not only forgiven by God, we are even "now justified by his blood" (Rom. 5.9). How immense is the grace of God.

4. *A new covenant*. "The blood of an eternal covenant" (Heb. 13.20) which the Lord Jesus had shed causes us believers to enter into a new covenant by which we receive its promised blessings, even the for-

giveness of all sins. The "blood of the new covenant" was once "poured out for many unto remission of sins" (Matt. 26.28 mg.). How marvelous that the work of substitutionary death lays the foundation of our entry into a new covenant.

5. *Reconciliation.* "Reconciliation" means that there is no more enmity. When we were sinners we minded the things of the flesh and were at enmity against God, for the flesh "is not subject to the law of God, neither indeed can it be" (Rom. 8.7). Insubjection is rebellion which in turn makes us an enemy with no hope of peace. But Christ died for us, and thus "we have peace with God through our Lord Jesus Christ" (Rom. 5.1); for "while we were enemies, we were reconciled to God through the death of his Son" (Rom. 5.10). Peace is the outcome of substitutionary death on the cross: "having made peace through the blood of the cross" (Col. 1.20).

6. *Are made nigh to God.* The gospel is preached to all who are afar off as well as to those who are nearby. For sin has separated men from God. During such period of separation men have no God, no Christ, no eternal life, and no hope. They are bound to sin. But Christ "through the cross [has] slain the enmity" that He "might reconcile them . . . unto God" (Eph. 2.16). Those who "once were far off are made nigh in the blood of Christ" (Eph. 2.13). Without reconciliation there can be no drawing near to God. First be reconciled, then draw nigh. This is truly grace upon grace.

7. *Ransomed.* Men were originally bound by the world, being enemies of God, living in the lusts of the flesh, having been sold and enslaved to sin, captured

and ruled by the devil who had the power of death, being always in fear of death, and by nature were children of wrath. Under such situation Christ came to redeem us—yet "not with silver or gold, . . . but with [his] precious blood" (1 Peter 1.18-19). People in the Old Testament time were redeemed with silver and gold, but Christ in obtaining "eternal redemption" (Heb. 9.12) used His blood to "purchase us" back to God (Rev. 5.9): "we have our redemption through his blood" (Eph. 1.7, cf. Col. 1.14). "His own blood" is indeed the ransom price He paid to "purchase" the "church of God" (Acts 20.28 mg.).

8. *Sanctification.* Sanctification is made possible through the death of the Lord. In His death all the Adamic nature in the saints died in Him. The old life was put to an end, even as the Scriptures intimate: that "he [Jesus] might sanctify the people through his own blood" (Heb. 13.12); otherwise, we can never participate in God's holiness.

9. *Can overcome the devil.* "Having despoiled the principalities and the powers, he [Christ] made a show of them openly, triumphing over them in it [that is, in the cross]" (Col. 2.15). "Through death he [Christ] might bring to nought him that had the power of death, that is, the devil" (Heb. 2.14). In His substitutionary death Christ overcame the devil so that by His blood we too can overcome him (Rev. 12.11).

10. *Shall not perish.* The Antichrist is labeled by the Scriptures as "the son of perdition" (2 Thess. 2.3). All who follow him will one day perish just like him. This is eternal perdition. Although the children of Israel were the chosen people of God, they had sinned just as

had the other descendants of Adam. They rejected their Messiah and had Him put to death, yet the Lord Jesus died "for the people" in order "that the whole nation perish not" (John 11.50). Sinful as the children of Israel were, they could also receive grace and not perish.

11. *Gentiles receive grace.* The Gentiles in the flesh "were at that time separate from Christ, alienated from the commonwealth of Israel, and strangers from the covenants of the promise, having no hope and without God in the world" (Eph. 2.12). But Christ has died "for the nation [of Israel]; and not for [that] nation only, but that he might also gather together into one the children of God that are scattered abroad" (John 11.52). Indeed, this is what the Lord himself has said: "And other sheep I have, which are not of this fold [sheep pen of the Jews]; them also I must bring, and they shall hear my voice; and there shall be one flock, one shepherd" (John 10.16 mg.).

12. *Deliverance from the present evil world.* The things in this age are all arrayed against the plan of God. Men cannot please God by doing things according to this age. But Christ "gave himself for our sins, that he might deliver us out of this present evil world" (Gal. 1.4).

13. *A cleansed conscience.* The works of men do not originate from the spirit. Though these works might be approved and admired by the world, they are dead. Dead works often carry the fear of condemnation and burden. But the Lord Jesus has died and His blood cleanses our conscience from dead works (Heb. 9.13-14).

14. *Can draw near to God.* The holiest of all in the tabernacle and temple was where men could commune with God. Originally only the high priest entered into it once a year. But the Lord Jesus has died for us. At His death, the veil in the temple that separated men from the holiest of all was rent in two from top to bottom. It was not rent from left to right, neither from right to left, nor from bottom to top. If so, this could be the work of men. But it was rent from top to bottom, for God had provided a propitiation. With Jesus' shed blood a new and living way was opened so that all who trust in His blood might boldly enter into the holiest of all (Heb. 10.19-20) and commune with God.

15. *Glory.* The death of Christ causes the believers to obtain glory. To be kings and priests are honorable things. All these come through the blood of Christ (Rev. 1.5-6).

The outcome of the work of our Lord on the cross is truly beyond numbering. May the Lord forgive me, for my foolish pen does not know how to present adequately the incomparable results of His substitutionary death. Nevertheless, we may sum up by saying that on the cross of Calvary the Lord Jesus has accomplished salvation. And once accomplished, it is forever completed. No works of men can be added. Whoever accepts God's salvation by faith shall possess it.

Hence, the grand total of the outcome of Christ's substitutionary death is—salvation. In his substitutionary death, three significant things are revealed, and these constitute the blueprint of salvation. The outcome of substitutionary death reveals these three significant facts:

(1) *Love.* Why did God send His Son to die for the world? None other than because of love! "God so loved the world, that he gave his only begotten Son" (John 3.16). "Hereby know we love, because he laid down his life for us" (1 John 3.16). The reason why the Lord Jesus came to the world is because God loved us. The restrictions, tribulations and persecutions He suffered during His earthly days of thirty-odd years demonstrate to us the love of God. His death on the cross for the sin of the world marks the peak of God's love. So that the preaching of the gospel of the cross is the preaching of the gospel of God's love. The love expressed on the cross is indeed amazing love.

Why did God love the world so much? I suppose no mortal can answer this question. Why did God love the world? Is it because the world is lovely? No. Then, why? God loved the world for no apparent reason. All we know is, "God so loved the world." Out of the fullness of God's merciful and gracious breast flows spontaneously the love towards unlovely men. Who can measure the length, width, height and depth of this love?

"Herein was the love of God manifested in us, that God hath sent his only begotten Son into the world that we might live through him. Herein is love, not that we loved God, but that he loved us, and sent his Son to be the propitiation of our sins" (1 John 4.9-10). "God commendeth his own love toward us, in that, while we were yet sinners, Christ died for us" (Rom. 5.8).

Hence, the substitutionary death of the Lord for sinners manifests the love of God.

The death of the Lord Jesus is not a martyr's death, nor is it an exemplary death to serve as a moral standard. His death is substitutionary for sinners so as to demonstrate God's love for them. From the cross God reveals His heart of love for the world. The message of the cross is God's declaration of His loving sinners. All who have accepted this measureless love cannot help but declare with Paul: "the Son of God . . . loved me, and gave himself up for me" (Gal. 2.20). Everyone should have this experience of knowing that Christ loved him and gave himself up for him. The Church that is redeemed by the precious blood of the Lord ought to praise Him without ceasing. For "Christ also loved the church, and gave himself up for it" (Eph. 5.25).

How very difficult for people to believe that God loves them. This is because being under the hand of the devil they hardly know what love is. "Does God love me?" "Yes, God loves you." "I do not see His love." "The Lord Jesus died for you. This manifests the fact that God loves you." Indeed, the substitutionary death on the cross reveals God's love.

> *Amazing love and exceeding grace of God,*
>   *The Holy Son volunteered to be a man.*
>
> *Substituting in the Father's glorious form,*
>   *Crucified and suffered terrible death.*
>
> *Deep is the compassion of God's Holy Son,*
>   *The dear Lord gave His life on the tree.*

Eternity is ages without end. Yet God's love manifested on the cross cannot be fully comprehended even with eternity. Many fancy that dwelling too long in heaven will create boredom for them. Let me say, truly, that although eternity is long, the love of Christ is even longer. How can any boredom set in when we will daily be filled with His fresh love?

Do you know His substitutionary death? Have you received His love? I hope you will sing with me in eternity, "Worthy is the Lamb that hath been slain to receive the power, and riches, and wisdom, and might, and honor, and glory, and blessing" (Rev. 5.12).

(2) *Sin*. The problem of "sin" is totally resolved on the cross. Because of sin, the world departed from God. Because of sin, God must punish the world. Viewing from their natural constitution, all men are sinners, since they are all born of the flesh and are descendants of Adam. But the Lord Jesus was obedient unto death, even the death of the cross. And "as through one man's disobedience the many were made sinners, even so through the obedience of the one shall the many be made righteous" (Rom. 5.19).

Viewing from their works, all men are likewise sinners. "There is none righteous, no, not one" (Rom. 3.10). Their thoughts, their works and their words are all sinful. But the Lord Jesus died for men's sin: "Him who knew no sin he [God] made to be sin on our behalf" (2 Cor. 5.21); "Christ also suffered for sins once, the righteous for the unrighteous" (1 Peter 3.18). Therefore, all who believe in Him are no longer sinners.

Finally, viewing from God's judgment, once again, all men are sinners. The word of God has encircled all in sin. From God's heavenly viewpoint, all are sinners. But the Lord Jesus died on the cross for mankind. He received the deserved judgment. Therefore, all who believe in Him shall not be judged.

In dying on the cross the Lord Jesus has resolved all the problems related to sin, even as the Scriptures tell us: "Him who knew no sin [was] made to be sin" (2 Cor. 5.21); "who his own self bare our sins in his body upon the tree" (1 Peter 2.24); "Christ also suffered for sins once" (1 Peter 3.18); ". . . the offering of the body of Jesus Christ once for all. . . . But he . . . offered one sacrifice for sins for ever . . . There is no more offering for sin" (Heb. 10.10-18); and, "He is the propitiation for our sins; and not for ours only, but also for the whole world" (1 John 2.2).

Therefore, we now can shout: "Behold, the Lamb of God, that taketh away the sin of the world!" (John 1.29) By the cross God announces to the world that He loves men but He hates sin. He himself has provided men with the way of salvation. The sting of death has been removed. Sin must be punished, but now the Lord Jesus has taken upon himself the penalty of sin in our stead. All who want to be saved can be saved. It is not the sinners who conceive a way of taking away sin; it is God himself who prepares the way of forgiveness of sin. Because of His love, He paid a heavy price for the world. He has resolved the problem of sin and is now stretching His loving hands to receive sinners.

(3) *Righteousness*. The cross reveals not only God's love but also His righteousness. The death of the Lord Jesus has fulfilled God's law as well as redeemed men from their sin. Propitiation expresses His love, while

the fulfillment of law shows forth His righteousness. Through the death of the Lord Jesus all problems of sin are resolved, and God's great love is thus manifested. Through His death the love that God has manifested is proven to be righteous love.

"Whom God set forth to be a propitiation, through faith, in his blood, to show his righteousness because of the passing over of the sins due aforetime, in the forbearance of God; for the showing, I say, of his righteousness at this present season: that he might himself be just, and the justifier of him that hath faith in Jesus" (Rom. 3.25-26). Verse 25 speaks of the sins committed before the cross, and verse 26 refers to those committed after the cross. Both the sins before and the sins after the cross have been fully judged on Calvary by God, according to righteousness.

God cannot ignore sin and treat it as nothing. Else this would destroy all measure of righteousness. Though He loves the world dearly, He nonetheless hates sin deeply. Though He is full of mercy, He still has His personal righteousness to maintain. Hence He will judge sin and yet He will love sinners. On the one hand, He will have His righteous demand fully met; on the other hand, He will give grace to sinners. The two sides are opposites and hard to be reconciled. Can God wipe away the sin of His created beings? On the one hand, He can; on the other hand, He cannot, because He has to resolve the problem of His righteousness.

The death of the cross is the solution to the dilemma. Through the cross God manifests His love: He "passes over the sins done" and at the same time He "shows his righteousness"; He "himself [is] just" and "the justifier" of sinners. On the one side, by the cross God has fully punished sin, condemned it, and executed the proper penalty. Thus His righteous demand is satisfied. On the other side, through the substitutionary death of the cross God can now forgive sinners, justify them, and set them free. Herein God's love is also manifested.

God is righteous, therefore He must punish sin. The Holy Son Jesus received upon himself God's righteous judgment in His substitutionary death on the cross. Now the righteous God may give grace to sinners, because His righteous demand has been met. There is now no more condemnation to those who believe in the Lord Jesus.

The death of the Lord Jesus on the cross has resolved all these issues of sin, love, and righteousness. The effect of Christ's substitutionary death reveals that the true God loved the world so much that He sent His Son to die as a substitute. It also reveals that God is most righteous, and thus He must punish sin. God deeply hates sin, but because He is merciful as well as righteous, He gives himself in the person of His Son who receives upon himself the penalty of sin. Now, all who believe in the Lord shall be saved.

5 | Why Christ Died

Why did Christ die? Die for men? or die for a cause? Here I have no intention to enter into theological disagreements, for such disputes are useless and vain. I merely want to turn the light of the Scriptures on the death of the Lord Jesus to see whether it is substitutionary or but a martyr's death such as the so-called "social gospelers" advocate. Nowadays there are many who preach a social gospel and exhort people to imitate Christ whom they honor as one of the best teachers in the world.

When they talk about the death of the Lord Jesus, they say that He was crucified because of the opposition of the people of that time to the doctrine He preached and the cause He embraced. He drew down upon himself the suspicion and jealousy of the world. And so to these social gospelers, His death was dying for a cause. To them His death is most admirable, and most fitting to serve as the people's model. Now what they say has some merit, but to deem the death of the

Lord Jesus to be *only* a martyr's death wipes away all the value of His atonement which is mankind's only hope of salvation.

From the scriptural standpoint these people are clearly the enemies of the cross. Their end, declares the Bible, is perdition (Phil. 3.18-19). The death of the Lord Jesus without question possesses the quality of martyrdom and is certainly fit to be a human model. But the purpose of His death was to die for the world in order to redeem it. Whoever questions the death of Christ as not being substitutionary in nature, that person remains a pitiful sinner. If any reader cannot properly answer the question, "Why did Christ die?", then I wonder if he is saved.

Let me answer decisively, "The death of Christ is substitutionary, for He died in the sinners' stead in order to atone for their sins." This, in fact, is what the epistles in the New Testament present.

1. *The Epistle to the Romans*

"Whom [Christ Jesus] God set forth to be a propitiation, through faith, in his blood" (3.25). Does it say here that the Lord Jesus died to serve as a model for men? Not at all. He died because God set Him forth to be a propitiation (or satisfaction) for sin. The meaning of Christ's death was not that He died because men murdered Him. No, the value of His death lay in His having been a propitiation to reconcile men back to God.

"Who [Christ Jesus] was delivered up for our trespasses" (4.25). He "was delivered"—this was a passive act. Who delivered the Lord Jesus to the Jews? Who delivered Him to the Romans? None other than God himself. No earthly person could have delivered Him to men to be crucified; God alone could. His death was not masterminded by men but by God. How unreasonable it is to assume that the death of the Lord Jesus was but that of a martyr. Furthermore, His having been delivered up was not due to His own sin (for He was sinless), but for "our trespasses." Is not this "substitution"?

"While we were yet weak, in due season Christ died for the ungodly" (5.6). We who should die need not die because Christ has died *for* us. Again substitution is in view here.

"While we were enemies, we were reconciled to God through the death of his Son" (5.10). If the death of the Lord Jesus only serves as an example to men, could men be reconciled to God by His death? A student cannot say to his teacher, "Though my penmanship is not good, the calligraphy book I copy with is good, so I deserve a good mark." However good the calligraphy book may be, it does not guarantee the copier a full mark. Christ died, and through Him we are reconciled to God. His death must have done something towards God so that we could be reconciled to God through His death. This proves that His death is basically propitiatory, not solely martyrish, in character. If a martyr's death could cause people to be reconciled to God, then many are the martyrs throughout the centuries. Yet can we be saved through them? Certainly not, "for neither is there any other name under heaven, that is given among men, wherein we must be saved" (Acts 4.12).

"The death that he died, he died unto sin once"

(Rom. 6.10). "Died unto sin" here has reference to doing away with the body of sin. For the death of our Lord is to take away sin. His was not the ordinary death of an ordinary person. He did not die for any cause He might have proclaimed (there was, of course, none proclaimed by Him); He died to bring to nought the old Adamic sinful nature.

"God, sending His own Son in the likeness of sinful flesh and (as an offering) for sin" (8.3 mg.). Here the Son of God is said to have been an offering or sacrifice for sin. According to the Old Testament, all sin offerings died for the offerers. When did the Lord Jesus become a sin offering for men? Naturally at His crucifixion. Except the sin offering has died, there can be no atonement. Does it not plainly say here that the death of the Lord Jesus is to atone for sin? This verse fragment alone is sufficient to prove that His death was not a martyrdom but a propitiation.

"Who is he that condemneth? It is Christ Jesus that died . . ." (8.34). The question here infers that none can condemn a believer for his sins. The sentence following answers why no one can condemn. And why not? Because the Lord Jesus has died. Why did He die? And what are the consequences of His death? That the believer shall not be condemned. All who are not prejudiced (leaving aside those who have no knowledge of substitutionary death) would agree that His death is different from an ordinary one. Moreover, it is different from a martyr's death. For the latter will not have the effect of causing people to be saved. The death of Jesus Christ is substitution in character. He died for men in order to atone for their sins. Hence all who believe in His substitutionary death and accept its accomplishment shall not bear their own sins. None can therefore condemn any believer.

"Him for whom [a believer] Christ died" (14.15). This cannot be plainer! It says "for whom Christ died." It must therefore be a substitutionary death.

2. *The First Epistle to the Corinthians*

"Our passover also hath been sacrificed, even Christ" (5.7). Christ became the Paschal (Passover) Lamb for the believers. When the children of Israel were about to leave Egypt, God decided to judge all the firstborns there. The firstborns of Israel were as much in danger as those of the Egyptians. But God prepared a salvation for Israel. He commanded them to kill a lamb and put the blood on the doorposts and the lintel of their homes. When the angel of destruction saw the blood, he was to pass over the house. All the firstborns of the Egyptians were killed, but all the firstborns of the Israelites were saved. Why? Let us see that there was death on both sides: Among the Israelites, the lambs died. Among the Egyptians, the people died. The lambs died for the firstborns of the Israelites. Thus the meaning of our Lord being called the Paschal Lamb is that He died for us. And hence we ourselves need not die.

"For whose sake [that is, for the sake of a weak believer] Christ died" (8.11). His death is substitutionary. In Chapter 11, a discussion there of "the Lord's Supper" is clearly a great testimony to the substitutionary death of Christ. His death was indeed substitutionary. Otherwise, how could His body and His blood be eaten and drunk? And how could those who do not discern the Lord's body and His blood be judged?

"I delivered unto you first of all that which also I received: that Christ died for our sins according to the scriptures" (15.3). Is not this scripture verse plain? Christ died for our sins. This is substitution. He died for sinners. This is what God's word records. God's word expresses God's thought. God therefore considers the death of the Lord Jesus as substitutionary. Here in His word He clearly says that the Lord Jesus died for men. Hence all who claim that His death is not substitutionary are enemies of God. We should not listen to them. The apostle stated here, "I delivered . . . that which also I received." And the first thing mentioned is the substitutionary death of the Lord Jesus. The "gospel" (1 Cor. 15.1) is first of all the fact that the Lord Jesus died for men. Accordingly, all who say that the Lord Jesus did not die for men but died to set an example for men are enemies of the gospel. We should reject their misrepresentation.

3. *The Second Epistle to the Corinthians*

"One [the Lord Jesus] died for all" (5.14). In its declarations the Bible never blows an uncertain trumpet sound. Everywhere throughout its pages there is confirmed the fact that Christ died for men.

"He died for all, . . . unto him who for their sakes died" (5.15). The Bible affirms that the substitutionary death of the Lord Jesus is a fact. It calls Him the One who for their sakes died. His death being substitutionary is indisputable.

"Him who knew no sin he made to be sin on our

behalf" (5.21). We have sinned, but Christ is sinless. Yet the Sinless One became sin for us. This is total substitution.

4. *The Epistle to the Galatians*

"Who [the Lord Jesus] loved me, and gave himself up for me"(2.20). What Paul maintained was that Christ did not die in vain. It is conspicuously plain that the death of Jesus is not purely a martyr's death. Since His death is able to justify men, how can it be merely an exemplary death? The death of the Lord Jesus is so meritorious that sinners can depend on it.

"Christ redeemed us from the curse of the law, having become a curse for us; for it is written, Cursed is every one that hangeth on a tree" (3.13). Here it explicitly records that Christ was hanged on the cross to become the curse for us that He might redeem us. Were His death of the same order as other martyrdoms, could there be any place for this kind of substitution?

5. *The Epistle to the Ephesians*

"In whom [Jesus the Beloved] we have our redemption through his blood, the forgiveness of our trespasses" (1.7). The Lord Jesus is the Son of God. His death is redemptive unto forgiveness. Does it say here that His death is to be an example to the world? Definitely not.

"Having slain the enmity thereby [that is, by the cross]" (2.16). Christ's death is His work, unlike with martyrs whose death is the end of works.

"Christ also loved the church, and gave himself up

for it" (5.25). "Gave himself up" shows His death was voluntary instead of it having been forced upon Him by men. Jesus died for the Church; and this was absolutely voluntary on His part. If He could *accept* death voluntarily, then certainly as the Son of man He could also voluntarily *reject* it. But a martyr, by definition, does not have that option. Is there not here another significant difference between His death and that of a martyr?

6. *The Epistle to the Philippians*

"He humbled himself, becoming obedient even unto death, yea, the death of the cross" (2.8). The Lord Jesus' death on the cross is an obedience to the heavenly Father. It is not because He had no power to resist arrest and its consequences. "My Father, if this cannot pass away, except I drink it, thy will be done" (Matt. 26.42).

7. *The Epistle to the Colossians*

"Through him [Jesus] to reconcile all things unto himself [that is, unto God], having made peace through the blood of his cross" (1.20). Through the death of the Lord Jesus on the cross men and God are reconciled. If indeed Christ's death is like the death of other martyrs, not only God cannot be reconciled through His blood, but the enmity between God and men will be increased because Christ, God's representative, was slain by men. But the Bible plainly declares that His death has accomplished the work of reconciliation between men and God. For this reason, His death must have redemptive value.

"Yet now hath he reconciled [you] in the body of his flesh through death" (1.22). Christ's death does not cause God to be at enmity with men. On the contrary, God purposefully sent the Lord Jesus to come to the earth and die at the hands of men that through His death the world might be reconciled to God himself.

"Having blotted out the bond written in ordinances that was against us, which was contrary to us: and he hath taken it out of the way, nailing it to the cross" (2.14). The crucifixion of the Lord Jesus is not just to set an example for men, for it has accomplished a *great* work: the Crucifixion took all the written ordinances of the law that were against us and nailed them to the cross. How could this be done? Because Christ nailed the law on the cross, and thereby He invalidated its demands. What, then, happened to righteousness? God would never destroy righteousness. In order not to destroy God's perfect and righteous law yet also set sinners free, Christ must fulfill in himself on the cross all the requirements of the law. Hence we read: "Having blotted out the bond written in ordinances . . . , nailing it to the cross." As He was being crucified, the Lord Jesus legally discharged all the demands of the law. Hereafter, the law cannot make any further demand.

8. *The First Epistle to the Thessalonians*

"Whom he raised from the dead, even Jesus, who delivereth us from the wrath to come" (1.10). The death of the Lord Jesus is intimately related to His salvation.

9. *The First Epistle to Timothy*

"Who [the Lord Jesus] gave himself a ransom for

all" (2.6). How very clear is this verse—that His death is to redeem man from sin. His death is a ransom for all. Because Christ died all can be redeemed. This is complete substitution.

10. *The Epistle to Titus*

"Who [the Lord Jesus] gave himself for us, that he might redeem us from all iniquity" (2.14). Here we are clearly told that the death of the Lord Jesus is "for us" and to "redeem us." "Gave himself for us" is a declaration of substitutionary death; "might redeem us" explains the purpose of such substitutionary death. Who can ignore such a distinctive declaration of God and not suffer loss?

11. *The Epistle to the Hebrews*

"Jesus, . . . that by the grace of God he should taste of death for every man" (2.9). He did not die for himself; He died to taste death for "every man." "Death" can signify being "alienated from life." In these terms "life" can serve as a figurative term for "God." And hence death is being alienated from God. According to man's fallen nature, he must not only die physically, he must also be alienated from God—and *that* for eternity. Separate from God's glory! Apart from God's presence! This is truly pitiful! How unbearable is this bitter taste. But Jesus Christ personally tasted death for each one of us. When He was on the cross He cried out, "My God, my God, why hast thou forsaken me?" (Matt. 27.46) How He truly bore our sins, suffered God's rejection, and tasted death for every man. How complete is this substitution and redemption.

"To make propitiation for the sins of the people" (Heb. 2.17). The soul that sins must die (Eze. 18.4). But Jesus offered himself as a propitiation for the people that they might be saved.

"Through his own blood, . . . having obtained eternal redemption" (Heb. 9.12). I sincerely thank God, for the Lord Jesus did not die for His own sake, but died for me. He has accomplished the great work of redemption. Once He died for sinners, He saved them forever. Here, again, we see that our Lord's death is not pure martyrdom; it is substitutionary in nature, since He shed His blood as a sacrifice for all. If His death be not substitutionary, then who had the power to crucify our most glorious Lord?

"A death having taken place for the redemption of the transgressions" (9.15). No one can change this verse into "Jesus died to be an example of great martyrdom."

"Once at the end of the ages hath he [Christ] been manifested to put away sin by the sacrifice of himself" (9.26). If His death be purely a martyr's death, then sin cannot be put away and the specific sin of murder must be pronounced upon those who crucified Him.

"So Christ also, having been once offered to bear the sins of many" (9.28). To bear means to bear the consequence as well as the responsibility of a certain thing. Christ died to bear the sins of many. In bearing their sins, He died for them. He is more than a model; He is the Substitute and Savior of mankind.

"But he [Christ] . . . offered one sacrifice for sins for ever . . . By one offering he hath perfected for ever them that are sanctified" (10.12-14). His death is meritorious. Mere exemplary death can never be compared with His death on the cross.

"Having therefore, brethren, boldness to enter into the holy place by the blood of Jesus" (10.19). His death is effectual in giving us boldness to enter into the holy place—that is to say, into the very presence of God.

"Wherefore Jesus also, that he might sanctify the people through his own blood, suffered without the gate" (13.12). He died to sanctify the people, not merely to serve as an example to men. In His death His work was done.

12. *The First Epistle of Peter*

"Knowing that ye were redeemed . . . with precious blood, . . . even the blood of Christ"(1.18-19). Everywhere in the Scriptures the death of Christ is proven to be substitutionary and redemptive. Apart from such kind of death, the word of God knows no other kind for Christ.

"Who [Christ] his own self bare our sins in his body upon the tree . . .; by whose stripes ye were healed" (2.24). Notice whose sins they were. Ours! And notice also whose body was upon the tree. Christ's! These sins were ours; so we should be hanged on the tree. Yet the sinless Christ was the one who hung there, and we were spared. And why? Because this is substitution.

"Christ also suffered for sins once, the righteous for the unrighteous" (3.18). Substitution! Substitution!! The unrighteous should die and the righteous should live. *We* should therefore be the ones to die, and Christ should live. But it was Christ who died. Is not this substitution?

13. *The First Epistle of John*

"The blood of Jesus his Son cleanseth us from all sin" (1.7).

"He [the Lord Jesus] is the propitiation for our sins" (2.2). This is substitutionary atonement.

"Hereby know we love, because he laid down his life for us" (3.16). This is substitution.

"He [God] loved us, and sent his Son to be the propitiation for our sins" (4.10). Again substitution.

All the above verses unanimously and jointly prove that God's Son Jesus Christ our Lord came to the earth to die for us that He might redeem us.

All the people in the world are sinners; there is no one righteous. The whole world should perish, because the wages of sin is death. Jesus came into the world to die for men. On the cross at Calvary He bore in His body the consequences of men's sin, even the judgment of death, which was due to us sinners. But also, He gave the righteousness, peace and joy which were His. This is not merely substitution but is also an exchange. He stood in the sinners' place and received the sinners' judgment so as to deliver them from perdition and punishment.

How very sad that many are propagating the so-called social gospel, a bloodless and non-atonement teaching which merely whitewashes the sinners into leading them to hell. They preach so-called social service, sacrifice and universal love, without giving any credit to the finished work of the Lord Jesus on the cross. Weep over it! Know that this is "a different gospel"—a kind which Paul remonstrated against: "which is not another gospel: only there are some that trouble you, and would pervert the gospel of Christ. But though we [including Paul himself], or an angel from heaven [the messenger of Satan], should preach unto you any gospel other than that which we preached unto you [that gospel which tells of the Lord Jesus, who died, was buried, arose, ascended and is coming again], let him be anathema [accursed]" (Gal. 1.6-8; see also v.9). Thank and praise God! Our Lord Jesus is not like what these perverters of the gospel preach. Rather, He is the One who loved us and gave himself up for us, that we might draw near to God and have the sure evidence of salvation.

I do not say that the death of the Lord Jesus is not exemplary enough, for there is surely no better model on earth. Nevertheless, His substitutionary death is the fundamental doctrine which God in His word has declared. Only those who believe in His substitutionary death and accept Him as Savior can begin to imitate His death. Believe in the *redemptive* Lord first, and then learn to follow the *exemplary* Lord Jesus.

Have you who read this received Him as your Savior? He loved you and died for you. You should accept Him and receive Him by faith.

6 | The Time of the Cross*

Each time we think upon the cross, we are amazed! Each time we consider how our Lord Jesus redeemed us, our hearts are filled with sorrow and joy. To us the cross of Christ is more than a wooden cross. It stands for the redemptive work of our Lord and the salvation that comes out of such work.

When I first believed in the Lord I often thought, how were the people of the Old Testament saved since the Lord Jesus had not yet been crucified? At that time I was a babe in Christ and was puzzled by this question.

Recently I have noticed very little refreshing power of the cross in the lives of many believers. To them the death of the Lord seems to be a distant affair—something which happened way back some nineteen centuries ago. Therefore, there is no more power.

---

*Unlike Chapters 1 to 5 of Part Two, the contents of this chapter appeared in Issue No. 3 of *The Christian* magazine dated January 1926.—*Translator*

I am really thankful to God the Father for He recently revealed to me especially about the eternal newness of the cross. I would assume that God's saints need to know the teaching concerning the "time" of the cross. Were we aware of the ever newness of the cross, how much more we would be moved by it.

The Relation of the Death of the Lord to the Old and New Covenants

Let us read Hebrews 9.15-17: "he is the mediator of a new covenant, that a death having taken place for the redemption of the transgressions that were under the first covenant, they that have been called may receive the promise of the eternal inheritance. For where a testament [in the original Greek, the word used is the same for covenant] is, there must of necessity be the death of him that made it. For a testament [covenant] is of force where there hath been death: for it doth never avail while he that made it liveth."

These verses explain the relation between Christ's death on the cross and the Old and New Covenants. During the time of the first covenant people sinned just as today. So, where there was sin there was the need of a Savior. For without obtaining God's forgiveness, sinful man must bear the penalty of his own sins. God cannot forgive out of His mercy alone, because this would make Him unrighteous. Hence in the way of God's redemption God established a substitution. During the Old Testament time many sacrifices were offered to atone for men's sins. When these numberless animals died for them, men could obtain God's righteous forgiveness. "Atonement" in Hebrew means "covered." All the atonements in the Old Covenant were effected by the blood of the sacrificed animals; therefore, they merely covered men's sins. For the Scripture plainly says: "it is impossible that the blood of bulls and goats should take away sins" (Heb. 10.4).

But when the fullness of the time came, God sent forth His Son to die for men. By offering himself once, Christ has accomplished eternal redemption. What sins the blood of bulls and goats could not take away (which were all of them) were all taken away by His death. For He is "the Lamb of God, that taketh away the sin of the world" (John 1.29). The death of Christ marks the time of a great transaction in history. His death divides the Old and the New Covenants. Before His death was the Old Covenant; after His death is the New Covenant. The scripture passage now before us communicates this to us.

These three verses in Hebrews 9 elucidate the twofold relationship of Christ's death to the Old and the New Covenants. Verse 15 tells us how He became our mediator, and verses 16 and 17 explain how He became a testator.

We have already seen how people in the Old Testament time were sinners. Though they offered sacrifices to God for atonement, their sins were only covered, not taken away.

Yet God did forgive their sins, for in the blood of many sacrifices God foresaw the blood of His Son and its efficacy. Nevertheless, without the death of the Lord Jesus the sins under the first covenant could not be concluded. Sin must be taken away. And hence, in

His death the sins under the first covenant were finally removed.

We may look at the relationship between the Lord's death and the first covenant from another viewpoint. Each covenant has its own conditions. The first covenant naturally has its own special requirements. When the requirements were not met, people committed sins. And the penalty was death. In dying to atone for the sins of the people under the first covenant, Christ fulfilled all the requirements of that covenant. And thus, He concludes the Old Covenant and commences the New.

Having died and atoned for the transgressions of those under the first covenant, Christ is now become the mediator of a new one. His being the mediator of the New Covenant is based on His atoning for sins under the first covenant. Originally men had the promise of eternal inheritance. Due to sin, however, they were not able to obtain what was promised. Now that Christ has died and sins have been atoned for, all who have been called may receive the promise of eternal inheritance. Thus, through His death on the cross the Lord Jesus becomes the mediator. On the one hand he concludes the transgressions under the first covenant and on the other hand commences the blessings of the New Covenant.

What has been explained is His being the mediator. Now we will touch upon His being the *testator.* "Testament" in the original Greek is also "covenant." Verse 15 of Hebrews 9 talks about the law of the covenant. Whoever violates its law must die. For this reason Christ died to redeem us. Here in verses 16 and 17 the testament of the covenant is in view. In the testament the testator specifies that after his death all the inheritance will go to the beneficiary. The Lord Jesus is the testator. All the blessings now and in the ages to come belong to Him. Just as He is willing to bear the transgressions which were committed under the first covenant, He is equally willing to give the promise of His testament to men. To expiate men's sins, He must die. To give us the promise of the testament He must also die. (For it needs to be remembered that as long as the testator lives, his testament is not in force; wait until he dies, and the beneficiary will inherit.) Thus, we see how deeply related is the death of Christ to the Old and New Covenants. Simply put, without His death neither the Old nor the New Covenant is complete. For without His death the Old Covenant cannot be completed because its lawful requirements are not fulfilled. And by the same token, without His death the New Covenant cannot take effect and the promised blessings cannot come to the beneficiary. But the Lord has died. He has concluded the Old Covenant and has established the New. Indeed, the New Covenant is sealed with His blood.

How Old Covenant People Were Saved

Since the blood of bulls and goats cannot take away sins, how, then, were the Old Covenant people saved? Through the cross. Men sinned; therefore, only by *man* can they be atoned. Although the animals were innocent and spotless, they could never expiate men's sins. Why, then, did God promise in Leviticus 17 (especially in verse 11) that these animals would make atonement for men's sins? There must be some profound explanation. Indeed, the things of the law were but "a shadow of the things to come; but the body is Christ's"(Col. 2.17). Hence all the sacrifices in the Old Testament time pointed forward to Christ. During the time of the Old Covenant (though Christ had not yet died), God reckoned all the sacrifices as types of Christ, their deaths as the death of Christ. In the profused blood of these sacrifices God saw the blood of His beloved Son. In the countless bulls and goats offered up He saw "the Lamb of God." In these many sacrifices He saw the substitutionary death of His Christ. In His acceptance of these many animal offerings, God in effect was accepting the work of His Son's death. Hence, men's sins could be expiated.

In reckoning these innocent bulls and goats as His dearly beloved Son, God could forgive the Old Covenant people on the basis of what they offered. Each time a sacrifice to be offered was slaughtered, it invariably spoke to God in type or picture of how His Son would one day offer himself at Calvary to obtain eternal redemption. Because Christ is a man, He can therefore atone for men's sins. But because He also is God, He can therefore propitiate Heaven for all the sins of the world.

Consciously or unconsciously the offerers throughout the Old Testament time believed in a coming Savior who would be crucified. Through these sacrifices they looked forward to a future Savior. Though the Lord Jesus was not yet born, faith saw the unseen, not the seen. Faith saw from afar a substitutionary Savior and trusted in Him. And in the fullness of time, the Son of God came and died for men. What they before believed now became fact.

How the New Covenant People Are Saved

We know we today live in the New Testament era. How, then, are *we* saved? Christ has died and salvation has been accomplished. If by faith we are willing to believe in the Lord Jesus—that is to say, are willing to accept Him as Savior—we shall be saved. Some may wonder how Christ could die for them before they ever were born. Indeed, from the fleshly viewpoint, there are many difficulties. But in the realm of faith, this constitutes a most glorious truth.

First of all, we should know that God is not bound by time. In the eyes of us dying sinners, several decades are deemed as quite a long period. But God is an eternal God. For Him, several thousands of years are as nothing. Though time might bind *us*, time cannot limit *God*. For this reason, we can be saved by believing in the Lord who died for us.

The Bible declares: "this [redemption] he [Christ] did once for all, when he offered up himself" (Heb. 7.27). He is God, therefore He could disregard the time factor and atone for the sins of people who lived thousands of years before Him as well as for the sins of people who would live during thousands of years after Him. Yea, not merely during *thousands* of years, even should the world unfortunately remain for *tens of thousands* of years after Christ, the efficacy of His redemptive work will still retain its power. For once He finished the work of redemption, it was forever done. Today, if a sinner wants to be saved he does not need Christ to come and die for him all over again. All he needs to do is accept the efficacy of Christ's once-for-all offering up of himself, and thus be saved. Like the people who lived before Christ came, *our* faith disregards time too; for like them it leads us into eternal reality. Just as the Old Testament people looked forward to a *coming* Savior, we look back to a *past* Savior. Yet by the term "past" here it is not to signify that something has passed away; it simply means that the work is done. The Old Testament people looked forward, we now look backward. If they by faith could accept a *future* Savior, why can we not by faith believe in a *past* Savior?

How meaningful it will be if in studying Hebrews 9 we can connect the three "eternals" to be found in verses 12-15. What the Lord has accomplished is eternal redemption; through the eternal Spirit He offered himself up without blemish unto God; and thus He causes us to receive eternal inheritance. Since what the Lord has accomplished is eternal redemption, whenever people believe in Him they indeed receive His eternal redemption. We know that the value of the cross is not determined by men. It is determined by God. God reckons the redemption of the cross as eternal in value. We, unrighteous sinners that we are, ought therefore to acknowledge God's word as truth, believe in the cross of His Son according to His word, and be saved.

The Time of the Cross

This is the focus of our attention. The Scripture does not just say that the Lord Jesus "had offered one sacrifice for sins"; it also says this: "He had offered one sacrifice for sins *for ever*" (Heb. 10.12); and just two verses earlier (and in many other verses elsewhere) it says: "we have been sanctified through the offering of the body of Jesus Christ once for all" (10.10). "Once" means that the Lord's sacrifice for sins is complete. Once He sacrificed himself, it is forever completed. His offering for sins is eternal: it is an eternal redemption. Not only is the *efficacy* of the Lord's propitiation eternal, the sacrifice He made is likewise eternal. Even though Christ has been resurrected and lives forever, the work of His cross is still eternal. Though He has risen, His cross seems to last forever. May we know the ever-continuing newness of the cross. It is not a past fact of one thousand nine hundred years ago. It is still new today.

"The Lamb that hath been slain from the foundation of the world" (Rev. 13.8 mg.). From the foundation of the world till now, and even unto eternity, our Lord Jesus is the Lamb slain. To Him, the cross is not an event which happened in a certain year, month, day and hour. It is to Him an event from the foundation of the world and continues on forever. When He created man, He foreknew the future cost of redemption. As the Lord used His power to create man, so He used His blood to redeem him. It is as though He had been crucified at the very beginning of man's creation. For thousands of years Christ has endured the sufferings of this protracted cross. The death at Calvary thus expresses how God in the Spirit has long grieved for the world, even from before He created the world. How marvelous! What grace! We really do not have the words to explain this wonderful verse. Even before He left the glory in heaven, God the Son knew the suffering of the cross. He knew thousands of years in advance of Calvary's event.

Thus from eternity the triune God had the cross on His heart. Using human expression, how it must have wounded the heart of God, who knew in eternity that the mankind He would create would fall into sin. But because of His great love, He foreordained Christ to die for us (1 Peter 1.20). Though Christ appeared once on earth to bear our sins, yet from the foundation of the world God loved us so much, grieved and suffered so much for us as though the Lord had already been crucified—and crucified thousands of times over! How sad that many today are still causing Him great sorrow, as though crucifying Him afresh to themselves (Heb. 6.6). But if we can see and appreciate such love, we will stand before Him amazed in silent wonder. Oh, this is truly God's heart! Should not we who see and know this love, love God more than ever before? Though from the human point of view we would say that the people in the Old Covenant period believed in a *future* cross and the people during the present New Covenant era believe in a *past* cross, in actuality the cross transcends time. The cross of the Old Covenant people is now. The cross of the New Covenant people is also now. May the Lord open our eyes to behold the timelessness of the cross.

The Newness of the Cross

People under the Old Covenant have already gone. We would therefore now turn our attention to the people in the present. Many today push the cross back nineteen hundred years. They view the cross as old, aged, and stale. Indeed, the view presented in the world's secular history is that Christ's Calvary stands as a past event. Yet in a believer's *spiritual* history the cross of Christ is forever new. It is not old, aged and stale at all. In that light, therefore, let us review several more passages of Scripture.

"Having therefore, brethren, boldness to enter into the holy place by the blood of Jesus, by the way which he dedicated for us, a new and living way, through the veil, that is to say, his flesh" (Heb. 10.19-20). To understand these two verses we need to know something of their Old Testament background. The former Jewish tabernacle was divided into two parts: the first was called the Holy Place; the second, the Holy of Holies. In between was a veil that separated them. Thus, to enter the Holy of Holies (which is actually what "the holy place" in the above verse has reference to), one must pass through a veil. God's glory rested in the Holy of Holies. Ordinary people could not enter it. Only the High Priest could enter in once a year. When he entered in, he had first to bring with him the blood of a bull and goat to atone for the sins of the people as well as for his own. Today, however, we enter into the Holy of Holies by the blood of the Lord Jesus. This is thus the efficacy of the cross. Formerly only the High Priest entered in once annually, but now through the cross of the Lord Jesus we believers can enter in *at all times*. What is the meaning of entering into the Holy of Holies? It means we can come before God to confess sins, to commune with God, and to be present with Him.

To have entered into the Holy of Holies, a veil must have been passed through. According to the above verse, this veil today points to the flesh of our Lord Jesus; for when He was crucified, the veil in the temple (which was the later-day tabernacle made of stone) was rent into two from top to bottom. Except the veil is rent, no one can pass through. If the Lord Jesus had not died and given up His flesh, no one could possibly enter into the Holy of Holies of God's presence. We now come to God through the death of the Lord Jesus. This, too, speaks of the efficacy of the cross.

The Bible tells us that the way through the veil has been opened for us by the Lord Jesus. Indeed, His willingness to give up himself redeems us.

We would next pay attention to the phrase "a new and living way." "New" in the original signifies "newly-offered" or "newly-sacrificed"—hence, "a newly-offered way." Thus we see the ever-continuing newness of the cross! The High Priest could not rely upon the offering or sacrifice of the previous year. He must bring a new offering, a new sacrifice. By the blood of these sacrifices he dared to, and could, enter into the Holy of Holies. How about us now? By the Lord's blood and through His wounded flesh we come before God. We have no need to offer a new sacrifice each time we come into God's presence. For our sacrifice is forever new! The cross of the Lord Jesus does not age through the passage of time. It is as fresh today and in eternity as it was when Christ was crucified. It never changes. Each time we approach God we can see the newness of the cross of our Lord. In olden days the High Priest would have been smitten dead before God if he had not brought with him the blood of the newly-offered sacrifice. For the sacrifice of the previous year could not have atoned for the transgressions of the current year. Unless God looks upon the propitiation of our Lord as forever new, we would all be consumed. Thank the Lord, the cross is ever new in the mind and heart of God. He views the cross as something newly accomplished.

This way is also "living," or as can be further translated, "alive forevermore." Hence, this way is an "alive-forevermore" way as well as a "newly-offered" way. We should therefore realize that Christ having risen, His resurrection continues to this day, even as we should realize that Christ having died, His substitutionary death lasts to this day. The two most significant things in the life of Christ on earth are His death and resurrection; for the efficacy of these two events achieves our salvation and leads us to God. Yet these two are not old facts but are new even up to this very day. Having such an ever-new Redeemer, we ought to accept Him, and through Him come to God and obtain His forgiveness and blessing.

Revelation 5.6 records how John saw the Lord Jesus Christ in heaven: "I saw in the midst of the throne and of the four living creatures, and in the midst of the elders, a Lamb standing, as though it had been slain" (in the original, "as though newly slain"). At the time that John saw the Lord in heaven, many years had expired since Calvary. Yet the Lord appeared as though newly slain. Oh, the cross is forever new! The cross outlasts time and remains new forever! If throughout all the time *in heaven* the cross is new, how can we ever deem it to be old *on earth* today? One day when glory shall be manifested in heaven, the glory of the cross shall never appear to have ever faded away! When all who are redeemed are taken to heaven, they shall see the redemption of the cross to be as new as ever.

One further point deserves our attention, which is, that in the Old Testament, Christ is referred to as a Lamb only twice (Is. 53.7; Jer. 11.19); in the Gospels and Acts, only thrice (John 1.29,36; Acts 8.32); in the epistles only once (1 Peter 1.19); but in Revelation, as many as twenty-eight times! The glory of the cross of the Lord Jesus shines throughout the ages! Especially in this book of the Bible dealing with eternity, God in His word makes a point of frequently calling His Son the Lamb. And the Lamb's appearance is as newly slain. His wounds are therefore externally visible! Eternal wounds guarantee eternal salvation. The crucifixion of the Lamb is to be our lasting remembrance. God never forgets, the angels never forget, and risen saved ones will also never forget the redemption of the cross. Who wishes to obtain this eternal salvation? The Lord's cross is the only secure place. All who have sinned, let them come.

The Remembrance of the Cross

God himself knows the eternal value of His Son's

cross. He also manifests the ever-new reality of the cross of His Son. He now wants all who are redeemed to know this too. Knowing the newness of the cross results in power, love, victory, and patience. If we truly understand this fullness of the cross, what revelation we will receive from it! How moved we will be! If in our eyes the cross is not old, what communion we will have with the Lord! In our forgetting the cross, we saints forget the Lord of the cross.

In order to make His cross forever new in our spirit and mind, the Lord says to us this: "this do, as often as ye drink it [the cup], in remembrance of me" (1 Cor. 11.25). "As often" means "always." The Lord instituted the Supper in order that His saints might often remember Him and His death. He foresaw that many would deem His cross to be old. Hence He commanded His disciples to remember His death constantly by means of the Supper. He knew how the affairs of this world, its many troubles and temptations, would gradually cause us unknowingly to lose the power of the freshness of the cross. For this reason, He commanded us to remember Him frequently in the Supper. When we first believed in the Lord, how very fresh was the cross to us! But after many days have passed, the luster and glory of His cross seem to be growing dim. When we first knew the victory of the cross, how new was His victorious cross to us! Yet after having heard much about the glory of the cross, strangely it becomes common to us. But the Lord does not want us to lose the newness of the cross. He wants to place always before us His sacrificial death.

Alas, we have lost the revelation of the cross of the

Lord Jesus. At all times Christ crucified should be openly portrayed before our very eyes (cf. Gal. 3.1). We should never treat the Lord's cross as a historical past.

The Epistle to the Galatians is a letter about the cross. How free the Galatian believers were while the cross was livingly portrayed before their eyes. But when they wished to receive the Holy Spirit by keeping the law and to be perfected by the flesh rather than by the Spirit, they lost the newness of the cross. The spiritual condition of a believer is judged by his attitude towards the cross. If ever he reckons the cross as old, he shall invariably lose the source of his spiritual power.

The Cross and Spiritual Life

What is the benefit of knowing the newness of the cross? It is indeed beyond description. We know that a new thing always excites us. A past thing, though, invariably seems to lose its grip on us. If we have the cross of Christ livingly portrayed before us daily, how much we shall be moved by it! Formerly Joseph of Arimathea secretly followed Christ. There was also Nicodemus who only dared to visit the Lord at night. But these two men were deeply moved when they saw Christ crucified. They dared to incur the wrath of the mob and even asked Pilate the Roman ruler for the body of the Lord Jesus for His burial. The cross transforms the most cowardly people into the bravest of men. When they beheld Christ on the cross enduring the assaults of the men He suffered for, they were constrained by the revelation of the newness of the cross.

Even so, if we always have the death of Christ before us, we too shall be moved as were they. The cross shall become our power.

"Shall we continue in sin, that grace may abound?" (Rom. 6.1) We must all answer this question. If we have really seen the Lord's cross on which He suffered, having beheld His painful face, His wounds in hands and feet, and His thorn-covered head, would not we be so touched that we would not dare do anything displeasing and hurtful to the Lord? It is because of a lack of the vision of the newness of the cross that we despise the love of the Lord.

If the reality of the death of the Lord Jesus is forever new before us, our also having been crucified with Him shall remain unchanged throughout time. If we daily have a fresh vision of the cross, our faith in our co-death with the Lord shall bring to us many new experiences. Due to the failure of daily seeing this cross, we fall into many sinful habits. Were we to see the newness of the cross daily as to how it remains unchanged throughout time, then reckoning ourselves as dead to sin would also remain unchanged.

Oftentimes we unwittingly fall. But let us thank God the Father, because He has not forsaken us for this reason. The Bible declares: "the blood of Jesus his Son cleanseth us from all sin" (1 John 1.7). He cleanses us not just once, but continuously; for the tense of the word "cleanseth" in the original conveys the sense of *continuous* cleansing. This is the eternal work of the cross. How good is the salvation which God has provided us! If we slip, we can come before God, confess our sins, and receive His forgiveness—

since the blood of His Son cleanses us from all sin. Oh, the newness of the cross!

Forever Saved

Knowing this causes us to shout aloud our praises to God the Father. How sad that many do not know they are forever saved. If we are saved, we are saved forever. Once we accept the atoning death of the Lord Jesus and trust in the work of His cross, we find His cross forever speaks for us. "The burnt-offering shall be on the hearth upon the altar all night unto the morning; and the fire of the altar shall be kept burning thereon" (Lev. 6.9). "Burnt-offering" is a type of Christ. The "altar" signifies the cross. "All night" represents the period of today's generation that is without Christ—the same as "the night" spoken of in Romans 13.12. Ever since the Sun of righteousness (a metaphor for the Lord Jesus, cf. Mal. 4.2) departed from this earth, the world has been in dark night and shall remain so until the morning—that is to say, till the Lord comes back. Yet, praise the Lord, the Burnt-Offering of God shall be kept burning on the altar all night until morning! Which is to say, that in this present age the redemptive work of the Lord Jesus pleads incessantly for us! In their day the children of Israel might have murmured in their tents during the night; but the efficacy of the burnt-offering that lay on the altar had burned before God continuously for them throughout the night! Let us realize that in our day, too, the Blood of our Burnt-Offering—even the precious blood of the Lord Jesus—intercedes for us constantly. The efficacy of the cross of Christ never ceases. Once we accept the cross, therefore, it pleads for us forever! And this is eternal salvation.

In the coming day, the cross in heaven will not become old due to the passing of time. Neither will our salvation ever grow aged. Eternity is never dull and lackluster. For as long as eternity is, it cannot dim the glory of the cross. For in eternity we shall see God opening up to us one by one the glories of the cross. Oh Lord! Teach me the ever-new quality of Your cross!

For what reason did the heavenly hosts praise the Lord? It was because of His cross, for we read: "Worthy is the Lamb *that hath been slain* to receive the power, and riches, and wisdom, and might, and honor, and glory, and blessing" (Rev. 5.12). In that day, we in heaven shall likewise praise the Lord Jesus forever because of His cross. Today the cross is the theme of the entire Bible. And in the future glory the cross will likewise become the reason for the continual praise offered up.

Oh, how new is the cross! It knows no time. It knows nothing of aging. May you and I be constantly constrained by it! Oh, may my whole life be melted in the cross! Oh, may it never for one day lose its power in me! Oh, may I allow the cross to do its deeper work in me every day! May God the Father open our eyes that we may behold the mystery hidden by Him in the cross of His Son. Yet "far be it from me to glory, save in the cross of our Lord Jesus Christ" (Gal. 6.14).

PART THREE

FAITH

1 | The Source of Faith*

Faith has its source. It is not in the saints; it is in God. If faith originates from the saints, how fragile must be that faith, and who then, can ever have faith? The sighs of many children of God are due to their lack of great faith. Not to mention having no *great* faith, some do not even have a *little* faith. How we wish to have greater faith in trusting God and allowing Him to work miracles in us! How we desire to have such practical faith that we can commit everything to God's hand without any anxiety. "If only we have greater faith, all will be right." This is our hope. "If only we had faith such as so-and-so has." This is our word of admiration. Have we not frequently asked the Lord to increase our faith? Why, then, do we still not obtain it? Is faith the sole possession of extraordinary saints? Is there any way for us to have greater faith? Of course,

*This appeared in *The Christian,* Issue Nos. 13 and 14, February 1927. —*Translator*

there is a way in the Lord, but who except those who receive can have it?

The cry of the saints today is for greater faith. But from whence does greater faith come? Unfortunately, the expectation of the saints is in *themselves* possessing greater faith. Can this be an error? Indeed, it is! The human error is in hoping to have in and by oneself this greater faith. No wonder believers do not obtain since they seek faith at the wrong source!

We usually ask ourselves, "Do I have faith?" "Can I believe God in this matter?" "Is my faith sufficient?" The answers to these questions are always "No." How this condemns us. Actually, we should not ask these questions. We ourselves are not the source of faith; therefore, we ourselves should not expect to have greater faith. The more we ask ourselves and the more we search within, the more we feel we have only a little faith or even no faith at all. And why? Because we ourselves are not the source of faith. Not being the source of faith, how, then, can we ever find faith by searching within ourselves? So we must now learn the lesson that we ourselves are not the source of faith. And as a consequence introspection cannot give us faith.

The word of God tells us where the source of faith is: "faith; and that not of yourselves, it is the gift of God" (Eph. 2.8). How very clear is this verse. Faith is the gift of God. So we know the source of faith lies in God, not in us. This may sound so common and so obvious to our knowledge. Yet few are those who truly understand the significance of the source of faith. Had we truly comprehended that God is the source of our faith, would we ask ourselves, "Is my faith adequate?",

"Do I have faith?" The very asking of these questions reveals that we are still ignorant of the true source of faith. Those who know will not pose such questions.

God is the Giver of faith. And hence, He is the source of faith. The meaning of God being the source implies more than just His giving us faith. It means we have faith, or increased faith, in God. In other words, the reason why we have faith or faith increased is because there is a certain quality in God that induces us to trust in Him.

What does this mean? It means we need not ask, "Do we have faith?", "Is our faith enough?" These questions become irrelevant. For these questions actually keep us in darkness and drive us to despair. What we *should* be asking are such questions as these: "Is *God* trustworthy?" "Is *God* believable?" "Will *God* relinquish His promise?" "Are *God*'s power and love real?" Our problem lies in always looking to our own side. Hence the more we search, the less we can find our faith. But if we can turn our attention to God's side, we shall immediately discover the faith that begins to rise in us. We ourselves are not the source of faith. No wonder that during introspection we could find faith nowhere! So, the more we look at the true source of faith—at God himself—and wait and meditate on Him, the more faith we shall have.

An illustration may help us to understand this teaching. Once a few brothers conversed with me on this subject of faith. Their feeling was that they had too little faith. I told them that it was not a matter of their faith being too little but actually their God being too small. For them to obtain greater faith they needed a greater God! I explained to them that day what faith is. Faith is committing one's own affairs to somebody else. If we believe in God it means we commit ourselves and our affairs to Him and trust Him to take care of them. I then asked them: When you commit *a certain thing of yours* to someone, do you ask yourself if you have faith in yourself, or have enough faith in yourself? Of course not. What you ask is "*Can* I believe him?", not "*Do* I believe him?" I then gave these brothers an example: Let us say that one of you is an employer. You employ a manager and commit the management of the shop to him. Now when you employed him, did you ask yourself: "Do I have faith?", "Is my faith too small?", "Do I need to increase my faith in him?" No, what you asked yourself was: "*Can* I believe him?", "*Is* he honest?", "*Is* he trustworthy?", "*Is* he believable?" If he was indeed honest, believable and trustworthy, you would have naturally handed over your shop to him. You did not need to ask yourself if you yourself had faith or whether your faith in yourself was large or adequate.

The same is true with trusting God. We need not ask whether we have faith or if our faith is great or adequate or if it should be increased. We need only to ask, Is God faithful, believable and trustworthy? We have no need to search within ourselves to see if there be faith. We will just naturally commit ourselves, together with our affairs, to God. And this is faith. Faith is not our own product. Faith is a reliance produced by the honesty, security and trustworthiness of the *opposite party*. So, then, what we contemplate is not a greater faith but a *greater God.*

We too often rationalize that due to our little faith we dare not commit ourselves and our affairs to God. The fact of the matter is that our hesitation in trusting God is not an issue of faith or no faith, little or great faith. It is because we deem our God to be untrustworthy! If God is faithful, why can we not commit to Him? If He is believable, why do we not confide in Him? If He is dependable, why can we not rely on Him? If He never "swallows" His word, why do we not trust Him according to His word? Perhaps the God we profess is unreliable, dishonest and unfaithful, and hence, we have no trust in Him! If so, then this is a time for us *to repent*! We dare to deposit our money in a bank which we know is honest and dependable. What each of us therefore asks is not, Do I have faith in this bank? Rather, we ask ourselves if the bank itself is trustworthy. A child in danger has no fear if he can touch his father's hand or his mother's face. He does not believe in strangers for they are undependable. But he believes in his parents for he knows they are trustworthy.

What we now need is not greater faith but the knowledge of the faithfulness and trustworthiness of God. Knowing God is the source of our faith, and in knowing Him we will not again search for faith within ourselves. Let us lift up our eyes towards God, learn to know Him and His believability. And then our faith will unquestionably be increased. If God is trustworthy, we will trust Him. If we do not believe in God, we are saying that He is undependable.

Our faith has its foundation, and it rests in God. What we believe is not ourselves, but Him. The problem with believers nowadays lies in their trusting in their faith more than trusting in God. If they feel *no* faith they dare not trust God or commit their affairs to Him; but if they sense there *is* faith they boldly entrust their affairs to Him. What is this? This is not believing God; this is believing in their own faith! We should not inquire or examine ourselves to determine if we now possess faith to trust God. What we should ask is, Is God dependable? If He is, why do we not believe in Him? If we should consider ourselves as having faith so as to dare to believe, then such is believing in our faith and not believing in God. On the other hand, if we should think we have no faith, and therefore we just cannot commit our affairs to God, then this too is not believing in God but is rather doubting our own faith!

Hence the problem is not with God but with our own selves. Indeed, you may not have faith; but does that mean God is undependable? Yet if God *is* dependable, why not trust Him? What you must be concerned with is, how God is and not with how you are. If God is believable, you just naturally will believe. Otherwise, even if you yourself have faith, it is totally of no value. For this reason, you do not need to trust in your own faith, since your own faith is not worthy to be believed in. But do believe God. "I know whom I have believed," declared Paul; and therefore, he added, "I am persuaded that he is able to guard that which I have committed unto him" (2 Tim. 1.12).

The Bible not only tells us *God* is the source of our faith, it tells us His *word* is the spring of our faith: "So belief cometh of hearing, and hearing by the word of Christ" (Rom. 10.17). Why does it say that God's word as well as God himself is the source of our faith? Here we see the wonder of God's word. How do we know God? By the word He spoke. His spoken words express His heart desire. By understanding His word, we come to the knowledge of what God has promised us, what He will do, and what He will not do. Indeed, it is through God's word, which is in the Bible, that we become familiar with His promise. According to His promise we believe in Him and ask Him in prayer. Without God's word, we will have nothing. For "how then shall they call on him in whom they have not believed? and how shall they believe in him whom they have not heard [concerning His promises]?" (v.14)

Will we not fall into superstition if we simply believe without having God's promise? Faith demands foundation. Believing without foundation is superstition. One will not be able to obtain what he believes. It is safe to believe what a father has promised to give because one's faith has its basis in the father's promise. But if the father has not promised to give and yet one forces himself to believe that he will give, this is dreaming, not believing. And why? because there is no foundation to what is believed. It is a person's supposition. Thus, we become aware of the intimate relationship between faith and promise.

God's promises are recorded exclusively in God's word which is in the Bible. To know God's promise, we need to know His word. Our faith is nothing if it does not have God's promise; and God's promises are documented in His word, the Holy Scriptures. Hence, "belief cometh . . . by the word of Christ" (Rom. 10.17). We mentioned before that what we believe is the faithfulness, believability and trustworthiness of God. If we know God, we will just naturally have faith. But this is also connected with God's promise, God's word. Without His promise, how do we know He is faithful? He must first promise, then He proves His faithfulness.

What is faith? Faith is executing what God has said and asking Him to work and fulfill it. Faith judges that God will perform what He has said. Faith believes in the faithfulness of God because whatever He says, He will do accordingly. Here the question is not concerned with little or great faith but with whether God will lie as to His promise. In other words, will He change? What is therefore to be asked is: Is God faithful? Is He able? The matter of little or great faith is totally irrelevant here.

We know that God loves us; we may therefore believe, without any doubt, that He is for us. Concerning His promise, the Bible manifests at least two things: (1) that God is *able* to do—"What he had promised, he was able also to perform" (Rom. 4.21). God is mighty. All His power is engaged in accomplishing His promise. Our God is not weak and powerless as though He can speak but not perform. If that were so, what would be the use of His promising? Would it not be empty words? But God has not only the power to speak, He has also the power to do what He has said. As He promises, so He is able to perform. "He can" is the revelation of the Divine Person: "the Lord hath power to make him stand" (Rom. 14.4); "God is able to make all grace abound unto you" (2 Cor. 9.8); "he is able to guard" (2 Tim. 1.12); and in the case of Abraham, he offered up Isaac because he knew that "God is able to raise up, even from the dead" (Heb. 11.19).

And (2), God has *the desire* to do. God is not only able to perform that which He has promised, He also has the heart to do so. Having the ability but not the desire will make a promise null and void. But God has both the power and the heart to do what He promises: "he is faithful that promised" (Heb. 10.23); "if we are faithless, he abideth faithful; for he cannot deny himself" (2 Tim. 2.13). As to what He has promised, God will perform to the letter towards His children. He *does* what He *says*. Otherwise, it would affect His deity, because God cannot deny himself. He is forever trustworthy. Should His promise be vain, we naturally could not commit ourselves and our affairs to Him. But God is faithful. He never swallows His word: He has promised, and where, then, is there any room for doubt?

Please do therefore learn this lesson today. You yourself are not the source of faith. Never ask yourself, "Do I have faith?", "Is my faith adequate?" These questions are useless. The more you ask, the less faith you have. Please go to God and ask Him what He has promised on this or that matter. Inquire of Him: Has Your love for me changed? Will You repent concerning Your word? Do You have the power to perform Your promise? Are You trustworthy? Are You dependable? If you think more upon God, your faith will spontaneously rise up without the need of manufacturing it. Do always remember this, that you yourself are not faithful, nor is your own faith trustworthy. God alone is the source of faith! And He is faithful!

2 | The Practicality of Faith*

The Bible contains many promises. All these promises are practicable for the saints to enjoy.

Our God is the richest and the mightiest. In various Bible stories we see what great works He had done for His children and how He stretched out His mighty arms to deliver, protect and guide.

God is forever the same. His words of promise are forever true. By seeing all the works God had done in the past we come to realize that all God's present promises are true. For all the promises in the Bible rest on God's power, love and faithfulness. Were God to change, all the promises in the Bible would vanish. On the other hand, if God remains unchanged (Praise and thank Him, because He *is* forever the same), then all the promises in the Bible will stand.

Saints nowadays have a mistaken notion, which is, that they do not expect God to work much for them.

---

*This appeared in *The Christian,* Issue No. 19, July 1927.
—*Translator*

Many think that the age of miracles has long passed. Nevertheless, the Bible is a *present* book; therefore, all the miracles in the Scriptures are not past events only. How many young believers, surrounded by the air of unbelief, reckon that miracles and wonders could only happen in Bible times. So now they do not ever expect to see these happening again. This is none other than rank unbelief. We ought to know that all the miracles included in the Bible can be repeated today. The greatest problem lies in the faith of the believers.

It is not because people pay no attention to faith. As a matter of fact, they always make mention of faith. We ought to believe, they say; but what really is important is how to believe.

Faith is real and practicable, it is not something abstract. Only in practice can faith be proven. We should not merely utter words of faith with our lips; we should also practice the faith we profess. For the subject of faith is not just spiritual terminology. "Faith is assurance of things hoped for, a conviction of things not seen" (Heb. 11.1). Faith is assurance, faith is conviction. Faith is a practical expression of genuine Christian life.

We often talk about faith. We exhort that men ought to believe in God. But how are we to believe? We are to believe God in our daily affairs. What is faith? It is a heart assurance that believes God in and for ordinary circumstances. Hence, faith is not something abstract or theoretical; it can be exercised.

If we believe God, we should not start to believe only when we encounter something extraordinary, something dangerous, or something beyond human power. Such is the way of the nations. It should not be practiced by God's children. For we not only acknowledge God as our Creator, we also draw near to Him in a father-son relationship. We ought therefore to receive His care and protection at all times. The power of heaven is backing us, thus causing us to conquer all things through God's power.

Now if faith is something practicable, then when is it to be practiced? We say quite naturally that it most certainly ought to be practiced at times of distress and danger. Yet it ought also to be practiced in life's ordinary circumstances. If a child of God cannot commit his body to God in time of sickness, who can believe him as one having faith? If a believer cannot trust God in monetary matters, where is his faith? If he cannot depend on God's arrangement in his occupation, the faith he professes with his mouth cannot help him. If at his work he cannot expect God to save souls but must rely on his own power and many worldly means, whom does he really believe in? Let us see that by faith we draw on all God's promises so that they may be manifested in our daily living.

God has promised, saying that He is "Jehovah that healeth thee" (Ex. 15.26). If that be so, will not believers avoid many medical fees by depending on him? Many profess they do not totally rely on physicians but instead trust God to use medicines to heal their disease. The problem is in the heart. Whom do we really believe in our heart? The acid test lies in a willingness to ask ourselves if we have the faith to trust God *only,* without using medicine. If we are unable to do this, our confession of trusting God yet using medicine has a tinge of falsehood about it. Whoever cannot simply trust God *without* the help of medicine cannot trust God *with* medicine, either. How often when in sickness and pain we seek healing outside of God without even thinking of Him. If we do not trust God in sickness, when *do* we believe?

Many dare not leave their present occupational positions for the Lord's sake. They are afraid they will end up unemployed by so doing. How short, in their estimation, is the arm of the Lord! Yet is it impossible for the Most High God to provide for you? Many faithful children of God have been tested in this area, and they know that their God is trustworthy.

Money is also a big problem. The Bible teaches, "Owe no man anything" (Rom. 13.8). Yet many are those who go for a loan as soon as they are in need. But surely, if we believe God and have a practicable faith, can we commit such an act against scriptural teaching? Why not wait peacefully upon God till He opens the way for us? Will He not take care of our food and clothing since He is the One who nourishes the sparrows and cultivates the lilies? Why cannot He who fed and clothed tens of thousands of the children of Israel in the wilderness under impossible circumstances provide for *you*? Is there no more manna or quails today? Actually God's food-bearing ravens fly everywhere (cf. 1 Kings 17.4). It is because saints themselves do not depend on God in riches or in poverty that they are unable to see what He can do for them. If we ever profess faith in God, our faith should also be practicable in our daily walk.

How manifold are the confusions and difficulties

which confront a family! Yet how few are the saints who trust God in family affairs. If *God* gives peace, who then can disturb? Why do we not trust Him? How often does a saint by faith commit his family matters to God through prayer?

If we truly believe God, why are we so anxious and perturbed in times of danger and distress? Is not our Lord sovereign over all things? If the entire *universe* moves according to His command, will He be at all short of ways to deliver *us*?

By examining our daily life, we shall readily come to realize how faithless we are! Lip faith alone can be of no service to us. Faith must be daily manifested in small things.

The Bible is full of promises. It has a promise for each occasion so that we may experience God's working for us. Simply believe and He will work.

3 | The Works of Faith*

Faith without works is dead just as works without faith are dead. This is true in the believer's life. We would here focus on Christians—that is to say, on the works of faith by those already saved.

The unique place to express faith is in our work. What we do expresses what we believe. If faith and work are not synchronized, our faith is faulty. Many believers do not know how to believe, nor do they know how to express their faith. As a matter of fact, it is very easy to express faith, for faith is manifested in works. In his epistle James the apostle said this: "Faith wrought with his works, and by works was faith made perfect" (2.22); and, "What doth it profit, my brethren, if a man say he hath faith, but have not works? can that faith save him?" (2.14) According to the teaching of Scripture, if we believe God in a certain matter, we

*This appeared in *The Christian*, Issue No. 22, September 1927.
—*Translator*

will exhibit a kind of work in that very matter. Otherwise, our faith will not bring in God's deliverance in that matter. Here we notice two things: (1) that our works prove our faith; and (2) that our works perfect our faith. Let us take up each of these matters in order.

The Proving of Faith by Works

With faith must come the corresponding *works* of faith. He who believes the house is on fire will not sit still inside it, else he simply does not believe. If we commit a matter to the Lord and believe that He will work for us, we are bound to change our attitude towards it. Believing that God will work for us and yet simultaneously planning and plotting with anxiety and worry shows that our faith is false: "we who have believed do enter into that rest" (Heb. 4.3). Faith and rest are inseparable. Whenever we truly believe, our heart is at peace. If our heart is still disquieted, fearful and perplexed and if we are yet struggling with planning, plotting, pleading and maneuvering, all these prove we have not believed. Faith is rest. Believe and you stop being anxious or diligently planning, because you are like a weaned child resting in the mother's bosom. Faith has its works. The first work of faith is to cease from one's own works and rest in the love, wisdom and power of God.

Such rest is most real and natural. It is neither pretended nor forced. Faith is restful because we know God is for us. "If God is for us, who is against us?" (Rom. 8.31) Thus is there rest. Having such rest is faith; the absence of such rest is not faith. All that is forced is not faith; only that which is natural is faith. When we see a person, we believe he is there. Do we need to force ourselves to believe? Do we need to convince ourselves of that fact with reasons and references? We believe spontaneously in a second. There is no need to struggle for faith. And real faith is always like this. Faith commences with God opening our spiritual eyes to see the reality of a thing. Since we have already seen and known, we just naturally believe. Faith enters into rest, yet not because it expects but because it knows. We rest in faith as well as believe restfully. Faith is most natural. What is not natural is not faith.

Of course, there is counterfeiting in everything. Whatever a believer's experience is, there is always the possibility of counterfeit. A believer needs to be careful lest he be deceived. And faith is no exception to this principle. Just here is where the problem lies: that many times Satan will deceive a believer by giving him false peace and false confidence that God will certainly work in such and such a way. But when God does not so work, this increases the believer's doubt and causes him to fall.

Believers ought to know that true faith is given by God for the sake of accomplishing *God's* will. Each time He gives us faith, there comes alongside evidence. Not in how we ourselves think or feel, but in what God has said. Sometimes He speaks to us through the Holy Book, out of which He expresses His thought about a certain matter and gives us a special promise. Faith comes by that promise. At other times He works in our spirit wherein He reveals His mind and grants His promise to us. As a consequence, we receive His given faith. God's given faith and His promise are inseparable. Yet, this does not mean the general promises to be found in the Bible, but rather specific promises given to you by God. Neither does this mean the sensations in your spirit, but whether the revelation in your spirit and the teaching of the Scriptures bear witness together to these promises. Only what God has impressed upon our spiritual senses with promises of the Scriptures is real, and the faith which comes from this is trustworthy. All real faith rests on what God has said, not on what we may think.

The Perfecting of Faith by Works

All that we have said thus far is to show that our works prove our faith. Let us now focus on how works perfect our faith.

When we believe God we naturally cease to worry or labor. This is the negative effect of the works of faith—which is something both essential and factual but not the whole story. With faith, there should also be the positive effect of the works of faith. The negative effect is not to work, but now there should be a positive working in the power of God. Our active works are to be in line with our faith. Such works will perfect our faith, enabling us to receive quickly God's promised blessing. This, however, is not the hastiness of the flesh; it only manifests the strength of spiritual power. As a matter of fact, God loves to supply our needs immediately; but due to the lack—or the shallowness—of the death of the natural life, His instant giving will only hinder the growth of our spiritual life. Hence God delays His promised blessing till our self-life is brought to nought. This positive effect of the works of faith deals a fatal blow to our self-life and it is a demonstration of spiritual strength. It speeds up the accomplishing of God's given promise. What are these positive works of faith? One such is to conduct ourselves positively as though we have already obtained that which God has promised. This is to take what is believed as that which is already done, and to act accordingly.

Let us illustrate it this way. Let us say you are sick, and God has personally promised you He will heal you. At such a time, on the negative side you naturally first rest in God, commit yourself—with your worry and sorrow—to the almighty hand of God, and refrain from using human methods to disturb God's working. On the positive side there is an important step to take, which is, that you should conduct yourself as though you are well. We are well not after we are truly well, but well after God has given us faith for healing. If we are well, we should have the action of being well. As we receive faith we should ask ourselves how a person who is healed by God would behave. Is he to lie in bed for long? or rise up and walk? A believer should assume the acts of a well person. But this must only occur after he has received God's promise and has wholly relied on Him. Otherwise, the result will be disastrous.

The same is true with our practical living by faith in God. Although sometimes we may be in lack, we look to the Fountain that never runs dry. We must not worry; we should not borrow (Rom. 13.8). We should still be generous in God's commanded giving and good deeds. If we trust in God, we should not tell people of our plight during a time of trials, nor seek out help by hinting around and by other suggestive ways. We should live as though everything is well.

With regard to those matters such as family peace, occupation, livelihood, tribulations, perils and other related issues, we should know that God not only cares for our spiritual affairs; he is also concerned with our earthly problems. Here is the uniqueness of faith. Faith does not wait to believe until after the thing is actually done, for at *that* moment faith is no longer needed. Faith is believing it is done after receiving God's promise but before it is actually realized. Such is the teaching of the Lord Jesus on faith: "Believe that ye *received* them, and ye *shall* have them" (Mark 11.24 mg.). It is not believing after having, but a believing of receiving *before* having. Here lies the mysterious way of the law of faith. As we have said before, faith needs to be manifested by works. Therefore, having believed in receiving, we ought to behave as though we have already possessed.

Such works are most natural. For the eyes of faith look not at the dark clouds of the sky. What they look at and see is the never-changing light of the sun above the dark clouds. *Fleshly* eyes will invariably see immediate darkness, but the eyes of *faith* see brightness of light. Faith is not conjecture; it is real sight: what it sees is shining light. Can it then be less real than the darkness seen by worldly people? Faith despises all dangers, trials and sufferings because it is aware of the final result. The works of faith are not risky but rather most accurate and practicable. Faith sees what people fail to see. Although people may consider it to be risky, such "risks" have been pondered and prayed about, as well as promised by God and taught by the Scriptures. If anyone confronts himself without having the teaching of God's word and the promise of the Holy Spirit in his spirit, he is really at risk. But for the one who has truly received God's revelation and has faith, he does it spontaneously without any pretence. This is the natural outcome of his faith.

Concerning faith, therefore, though its works seem to be contrary to human reasonings, it is merely operating according to its own living rules. It has received God's promise and has known the outcome; therefore, its works are simply those steps which are ahead of ordinary people. The works of faith always glorify God.

4 | Sincerity, Deception and Knowledge*

Spiritual knowledge is profitable for it gives us clearer guidance in our spiritual journey. Ignorance often leads us to error. The saints go astray because of the lack of spiritual knowledge. Satan always takes advantage of the ignorance of the saints to steer them into errors. The Holy Spirit is not afraid of men having knowledge (that is, spiritual knowledge). The more knowledgeable, the easier led. The devil is the power of darkness. He uses darkness, he loves darkness, and he keeps people in the dark. The less knowledge one possesses, the easier to be deceived by Satan.

Christians frequently embrace a misconception, thinking that in being sincere they cannot be deceived: as long as I am sincere in my heart, I will not be misled. Who would imagine that it is the sincere souls who are mostly deluded! Saints who are deceived by Satan

*This appeared in *The Christian*, Issue No. 11, November 1926.
—*Translator*

usually consider themselves as very sincere in their searching for faith. They pray, they study the Bible, they fast, and they diligently pursue after spiritual experiences. Even so, they are unable to avoid being deceived. They are unaware that Satan can easily inject a thought into their mind, causing them to think wrongly. They are also unaware that Satan can very easily put a kind of stubborn intent into their heart, causing them to hold on to what they deem to be the only truth. They fancy that since they so honestly seek after God's gift, they will certainly be protected by God from deception.

Who knows that God's protection has its conditions? If the saint does not work with God in strongly resisting Satan, in earnestly seeking for God's light on the matter, and in explicitly obeying the word of God, how can God protect him? God has not promised to protect us unconditionally. On the contrary, we must cooperate with Him to be protected.

Satan usually beguiles the saints by first suggesting to them that they will not be deceived. All who believe they cannot be deceived are mostly the deceived, the deeply deceived. The angel Lucifer turned himself into Satan because of pride. His working tactic is to make people proud of themselves, some openly and some in a hidden way. (Alas, sometimes the pride is so hidden that it causes people to think they will never be deceived, and they secretly pity those who do not possess their supernatural experiences.) Let all who vaunt themselves as beyond deception beware!—lest they fall into delusion. If we are humble and not self-conceited —acknowledging ourselves as possibly able to be cheated, if we seek with singleness of heart before God for the revelation of the reality of the matter, and if we wholeheartedly resist the works and wiles of the enemy, then we shall understand whether our spiritual experiences come from God or from Satan.

We should never forget that "even Satan fashioneth himself into an angel of light" (2 Cor. 11.14), and that "his ministers also fashion themselves as ministers of righteousness" (v.15). In spite of the fact that the supernatural experiences we have are very beautiful and seem to help us grow at least outwardly, even causing our hearts to burn with exceeding joy—such experiences as frequently speaking in tongues, having healings, seeing visions, knowing hidden things of mystery; even sometimes being so stirred by spirits from the outside that an intimate sense of the Lord Jesus comes upon us; that even in times of prayer the Lord seems present in the room so that there is no need to pray to God in heaven but simply to pray to the Lord in the room—we should not immediately accept all these as coming from God. Instead, let us acknowledge that we have the possibility of being deceived. Sincerity is *not* the condition against deception. Let it be understood that countless numbers of sincere believers have been deceived. There is no guarantee that we will not be deceived. We therefore need spiritual knowledge.

We should know something about spiritual laws. For God works along certain definite principles. Unless believers know and obey God's working principles, they cannot expect protection from Him. The most critical question is: Suppose our supernatural experiences do not come from God, are we willing to reject them? Let us not quickly assume that we are willing. For actually, there is probably much *un*willingness in our heart: there is the possibility that we love our strange experiences too much to let them go! Hence, before this critical question is settled, we shall not be able to possess the knowledge to move forward. But after this first step has been taken, of being willing, if need be, to let go of our experiences, then we can take the second step. This next step is to assume an attitude that if our experiences are not of God we will resist and oppose them. We will resist and oppose all which comes from Satan. We will also pray without ceasing that God reveal the truth to us. And thus God in His own time will instruct us and cause us to understand.

Before we have tested the source of our experience, and no matter how supernatural it may be, we must reserve our trust. In dealing with things in the spiritual realm, imagination and speculation are totally undependable. Except we have received in our spirit revelation from God as to the truth of a matter, unless we have definitely tested the matter as being from Him, we must not automatically assume that it is God-given. Without the knowledge from God, there is nothing we can believe. Our own sincerity will not keep us from being deceived. For us *not* to be deceived, therefore, we need to have God give us the knowledge of the truth.

5 | Cool Head*

Easy is it to have a cold heart, but it is hard to have a cool head. For our love towards the Lord and towards men to grow cold, we have no need to plan and plot for it. Just a little less watchfulness, and our love will grow cold in the twinkling of an eye. Not so with our head. Frequently, the more we think, the more we are confused. The more we think, the more we become hot in the head. When we are provoked, we lose our composure. Our heart should be warm, but our head must be cool. Coolness of the head signifies being unaffected in the mind by provocation. Saints who seek for perfect life must pay attention to their head.

Although the mind may not direct our life, it can at least affect our life. Without a cool head there can be no composure. Once the head grows hot, one loses his control. Let us be reminded that self-control is the ninth ingredient in the fruit of the Holy Spirit (see Gal.

---

*This appeared in *The Christian,* Issue No. 11, November 1926.
   —*Translator*

5.22-23). Losing our self-control means losing the fragrance of the Holy Spirit in our lives. As our mind becomes irritated, we unconsciously change our normal attitude. In such condition, we act as though being tossed by the wind and the waves, drifting without control. At such a time, our speech, action and manner become so ill-affected by the stimulus in our mind that we exhibit abnormal phenomena. And probably we even remain ignorant of it happening.

When we are composed we can easily detect disquiet or agitation in others. But when we ourselves are excited, we cannot see our own fault. In noticing what people do and say under provocation, we quickly condemn them, and judge them to be in the flesh. Yet when we exhibit the same symptoms under excitement, we fail to see our fault. Such is the difference between a head that is cool and one that is perturbed. With a cool head one can discern and evaluate things clearly and correctly. Otherwise, right and wrong will be distorted and misjudged.

This applies to ourselves as well as to what we observe in others. After we have lost—under provocation —our normalcy in action and speech, and after our "inflated air" has disappeared, our head gradually cools down. Then, in quietness, we recall our action under pressure and begin to laugh at our folly. We either deeply condemn ourselves or secretly feel ashamed of ourselves. When our head is cool we do not condone the things done hotheadedly. In returning to normalcy we do not justify the actions we took under excitement. What we committed when agitated is either sinful or unbecoming. For during this or that time of excitation, the more we thought about what provoked us the angrier we became. We came under the power of the flesh and thus fell into sin. At one time we might have mocked and jested unnaturally. At another time we might have spoken untrue words. Or our thoughts rose and ebbed like the tide. At times we might even have lost our sleep at night and our appetite during the day. Or we might have experienced sorrow at one moment and joy at another. We might have wished one way but walked another way. At one time we might have pushed with tremendous force and at another time have dragged our feet as though chained down with a weight of a thousand pounds. But when this or that storm had passed and we sat before the Lord examining ourselves in His light, we could not help but laugh at ourselves. How soulish we were!

As a matter of fact, we all know the stupidity of actions under provocation. Only when provoked or irritated do we have no power to control ourselves. For this reason, we must guard against taking such provoked action and keep our head cool. If we realize we are being provoked, let us each say to ourselves, "I am being provoked. I should not take action now, or else I will fall." Resist Satan and his wiles. Learn to be your *own* master at that time. Control the irritation and demand *its* submission. Each time we overcome, our strength shall be increased for the next victory. In case we do not realize we are excited, let us ask ourselves, "Is it because I am irritated that I speak and think and act in this manner?" If so, let us pray and ask the Holy Spirit to give us the strength to master the situation.

Let us control agitation or irritation instead of allowing ourselves to be controlled by it.

Provocation is the ready weapon of Satan by which he causes the saints (1) to sin (especially exhibit anger), and (2) to walk outside the will of God. A slight carelessness in this area is enough to disgrace the name of the Lord. During a time of changing thoughts and mounting emotions, let us not forget this. A cool head is the secret of maintaining peace. The loss of peace is largely due to a provoked head. Though peace is normally lost when one is under provocation, it is not absolutely impossible to keep the peace when provoked. As the cross revealed in God's word works deeply in us in dividing the soul and spirit (see Heb. 4.12), we shall have the power to fully control provocation when it strikes. We shall see that amid confused and perturbed surroundings our heart can remain unmoved: there *can* be inner peace. In such circumstances, a cool head is the condition for the Holy Spirit to lead us into doing the will of God. To become provoked, agitated or disquieted gives Satan opportunity to manipulate us into departing from the straight path. On the other hand, a cool head amidst such circumstance gives opportunity to the Holy Spirit to guide us. The Holy Spirit has no need or desire to utilize our confusion. He works, rather, in our quiet spirit, shining His quiet light into our mind that we might know what the will of God is.

Even the most spiritual saints experience occasions of being provoked. Unless we watch constantly, no one will be spared from the negative consequences which can so easily flow from such provocation. All who wish to follow the Lord diligently must be on the alert.

6 | Borrowed Experience*

Experience is very personal. What one has not personally passed through cannot be considered experience. All Bible teachings and spiritual doctrines remain as teachings and doctrines so long as they are not personally verified by experience. Experience is life, not idea. Our minds may be filled with many beautiful thoughts and ideas, but personal experience alone is the stuff of practical living.

One thing especially is to be lamented of, and that is, that the mental life of believers nowadays develops faster than their experimental life. In spiritual reality, what we *think* is not ours, only what we *experience* is truly ours. There is one class of Christians who themselves are short of deep experiences in the Lord, yet they are rich in the power of imitation. Not that they have no heart for spiritual knowledge; quite the contrary, they are most interested and pay much attention

*This appeared in *The Christian,* Issue No. 11, November 1926.
—*Translator*

to these things. Their hearts admire those who have experiences of the Lord. Although they themselves do not have much communion with the Lord, they nonetheless applaud those who have. They themselves lack that consuming love and intimate feeling towards the Lord, but they delight in the expressions and words of those who possess such loving relationship. They themselves do not possess such sure faith as to cause them to pray without ceasing and to receive number-less miracles and wonders as answers to prayer, yet they appreciate such spiritual experiences in others. Due to such inclination in their hearts, many preten-sions are being produced. Before they believed in the Lord and were born again, this class of people usually loved to show off, sought fame, were rich in emotions, and coveted glory. So that once they were regenerated and saved, they expected to make speedy progress in their spiritual journey, thus obtaining a name and glory among the rank of spiritual giants. We cannot say that their entire intention is directed towards vain fame and glory. In fact, their pursuit after spirituality is not behind that of anybody else. Nevertheless, in the secret place of their hearts (some more, some less) is hidden the desire for self-glory. This desire intensifies their pushing ahead in the spiritual pursuit; even so, they are rarely compensated.

The spiritual journey is made step by step, just as in a physical journey. True, those who faithfully serve the Lord—making no detour, having no drawback, and putting up no obstinacy but walking in perfect obedi-ence to the Lord—will be able to cover a rather long distance in a relatively short time. But those who are anxious to cover the distance in double-quick time by using their own strength and method shall discover that in the spiritual journey there is no shortcut! Frankly speaking, it is harder for this latter class of believers to make progress than those who are apparently slower. For what the slower believers do not possess is no different from what the anxious believers *appear* to possess. Neither have actually possessed anything.

In view of their repeated failures under the influence of the sinful nature, the slower believers tend to faint, considering themselves unworthy of spiritual maturity. In their view they can never overcome. This is indeed regrettable. Nonetheless, God can still deal with them and lead them on. Yet those who are overanxious are most difficult to handle. Their trouble with the flesh is no less frequent than the slower ones, and actually may be more frequent. They are constantly defeated, but their nature is such that they find it most difficult to confess their fall before men. Their craving for honor and renown is so strong, yet they can hardly make boast of anything because of their constant failures. When they are defeated they bemoan the loss of their glory before men more than they bemoan the transgressions they have committed. Though in their outward appearance they will not acknowledge that they are so greedy for glory, they are forced to cover over their outward appearance. By so doing, they fall into pretension.

The flesh of the overanxious and proud ones is constantly in rebellion, causing them frequent falls. Yet this does not make them humble. Due to their impure desire, they often borrow other people's spiritual experiences as their own without themselves having these experiences. They memorize others' spiritual sermons and at appropriate times release some words to gain the good name of being deeply spiritual and highly knowledgeable—yet unaware that what they say does not come from corresponding life and character. How unfit! They learn the spiritual vocabulary of those who have intimate communion with God and pilfer such as their own, but without comprehending that their spirit—yea, even their very appearance—is so unlike that of the original speakers. They also collect speeches of those saints who understand the world and its standing; then, as opportunities arise, they give these words out as their own. Imagine how their hearts must accuse them of their falsehood! They have frequently heard the stories of how people's prayers were answered. So, they search their own experiences and try to match them up with what they have heard so as to draw admiration. Yet in their very heart they doubt if God actually answers prayer! They have heard how people thank and praise God in tribulations, so they mimic the same. They praise with their lips but not with their heart, and therefore they are totally unacceptable to God. More often than not they adopt the spiritual words used by others in pouring forth longings for the Lord and compassion for souls. Of course they fail because while they are using these words in prayer their hearts (apart from having some emotional stirrings) are neither moved nor so motivated.

Sometimes, as we listen to lectures on the deeper life, our mind can fairly well grasp their meanings for they are so clearly presented. Yet just here lies a great danger for us. For we think that, because we understand, we possess the ways of the deeper Christian life; not realizing that at a critical moment we will become unfaithful and will not react as we have heard since we shall fail to cooperate with the Lord. This is all because what we ourselves have *not* experienced is indeed not ours, for what we only understand in our mind still belongs to others. We ourselves possess nothing in experience.

Borrowed spiritual experience leads us to self-pride and arrogance, we deeming ourselves to have reached the top. We covet glory, though such vanity causes us to fall. Borrowed spiritual experience will not help in our spiritual progress; instead, it poses a sure obstacle to our spiritual advance. One day at the judgment seat of Christ all which is borrowed will be manifested. Not a single pretension shall remain covered before His judgment seat. May we therefore be the instructed who are humble enough not to consider "I already know" as sufficient, but may be faithful to the Lord instead. Let us inquire of ourselves wherein we have truly arrived.

7 | Important or Unimportant*

How do we differentiate between important and unimportant? We frequently hear God's children say, This kind of teaching in the Bible is important and that kind of teaching is unimportant. How do we distinguish? What is important doctrine? And what is not important?

After careful observation, we would conclude that what many consider important doctrines are those related to their salvation problem. Those not related to salvation become so-called unimportant doctrines. How often we hear people say, "Do I have to obey the Lord in this matter? I judge this to be insignificant for it does not affect my salvation." Duller Christians even pose this question, "Does this concern salvation? If it does, I should obey. Otherwise, I am saved and what does it matter to me?"

Important to many are the doctrines that are con-

*This appeared in *The Christian*, Issue No. 19, July 1927.— *Translator*

cerned with believers' salvation; unimportant to them are those related to God's command and glory. Yet why are the latter unimportant to them? Because these do not have a direct bearing on saints going to heaven and having eternal life. It would appear that God's command and God's glory alone will not inspire saints to obey.

How pitiful that such is the condition of many saints. If God were to require men to keep all His commandments and to obey all His wills in order to be saved, people would be ready to keep and obey. But since God has said that whosoever believes in the Lord Jesus has eternal life, believers reckon that because they have already believed and possess eternal life, why be bothered about God's other commandments and wills? Apart from heaven and hell, nothing can move the hearts of the saints. Unless God sets before them all His commandments as conditions for salvation, He cannot expect His saints to keep them. For what these believers hope and plan for is nothing but eternal life and heaven. How to please God and to obey His will are out of the question. How truly pitiful this is!

Saints nowadays are most selfish. Nothing other than what is related to their own salvation can attract their attention. Is this what God looks for? He wants us to obey Him voluntarily. He does not like to coerce us. He loves to give us grace so that in believing His Son we might have eternal life. For this reason, He does not include His commandments as a condition for our salvation. Otherwise, He would be putting us under law. Unfortunately, believers do not behave as obedient children and they do not walk according to the Father's will. They ask instead, "Is this important to my salvation or is it unimportant?"

We would acknowledge that the doctrines in the Bible can be classified as primary and secondary. But we will not accept the notion that there is any difference in importance about them. If some were indeed unimportant, why would God be so uneconomical as to place many of these so-called unimportant doctrines, commands and teachings in the Bible? He should know better than to fill up the Scriptures with so many unimportant matters. Hence the question before us today is not whether any Biblical doctrine is important or unimportant (since it is written in the Bible, it *must* be important), but whether the saints honor God's glory and respect His will. For let us look at the life of the Lord Jesus while He was on earth. What can we say about it? Here He is, the Son of God who had no need to be saved. If that is so, then according to modern men's view, nothing should have been deemed by Him to have been important. And yet, while He was on this earth, how obedient to God He was! Even in the minutest matters He fulfilled all righteousness. Moreover, He never bargained with God as many believers today do in all those things not pertaining to salvation. Needless to say, we all need to imitate our Lord.

There is sometimes another way by which many saints distinguish between what is important and unimportant. This approach is highly personal and is defined as follows: what the saint has indeed kept is considered important but what he has not yet kept and obeyed is unimportant! Hence importance or unimportance is not determined according to the Bible but according to one's own criterion. Because a believer has already obeyed in a given area, that makes it important to him; whereas what he has not yet obeyed is pushed onto the back burner.

Alas, is not this the time for God's children to be revived?!? Surely this is the moment for us to revive our obedience to God's commands. May we pay more attention to God's glory and care more for God's will (even as Paul noted when he wrote in Colossians 4.12, "all the will of God"). May we not divide God's word into important and unimportant according to our own selfish considerations. We ought to realize that obedience is not only to obey in the big things but also in the small things. To rebel in a big matter is obviously rebellion, but so too is it to do so in a small matter. May we walk according to the commands of Holy Scripture and make glorifying God the fundamental motive in our daily life, regardless whether things be big or small.

Was the act itself of eating the fruit of the tree of good and evil in the Edenic garden a big thing? Yet eating in violation of the prohibitive command of God resulted in Adam's expulsion from the garden and became the root of all mankind's sins. Was the sin Achan committed a big one? What he had stolen and hidden away might not have been worth a lot; yet he rebelled against God. So, he received his terrible punishment of being stoned and burned to death. Why did King Saul lose his kingdom? What he had done might not be viewed as a frightening sin, it only being an act of disobedience in a small matter. Yet he lost his kingdom as a result. Moses, whom the Bible records was the meekest of men, could not enter Canaan. For what reason did he suffer such a penalty? Was it because he committed a great sin? No, it was only because of a seemingly small thing: Out of His compassion for the Israelites, God had ordered Moses to *speak to the rock* that waters might flow out to quench the people's thirst; instead, Moses in anger *struck the rock* twice. According to the view of men, what sin could that possibly be? In modern men's eyes such an act of disobedience would be regarded as quite unimportant—even perhaps justified. Yet it cost Moses the right to enter the Promised Land!

May we hereafter be more obedient to God! May we deem all God's commands important!

8 | Bribing the Conscience*

Conscience is the voice of God's righteousness speaking from within us. Conscience is an integral part of man. Its function is to reproach all which is not of God and His righteousness. Indeed, it can be likened to a prosecutor. It draws the line against which man ought not to trespass.

How fearful is a believer towards his conscience! He whose heart is upright will obey its correction and direction. But he whose heart is crooked will try to bribe his conscience so as to stifle its accusing voice. But can conscience be bribed? Conscience can never be bribed. Nonetheless, after a believer has bribed it, he fancies he need not listen to its voice any longer. Actually, at that moment the voice of conscience is only being confused and even drowned out by other voices.

Many a time conscience through intuition clearly

*This appeared in *The Christian,* Issue No. 24, December 1927.
—*Translator*

tells us where God's will lies, what His will is, and what He expects us to do. Yet how unwilling we are to obey. What the flesh fears most is God's will. It can be said that apart from the will of God, the flesh has no other fear. The mind of the flesh does not know God's law; so naturally it refuses to obey. Hence conscience must perform its duty to instruct. When instruction fails, it continues with accusation. How hard this is to the flesh! How uneasy is the heart if it allows conscience to work! How unbearable it becomes! In order to avoid the self-accusation of conscience as well as avoid obedience to God's will, a person resorts to bribing the conscience.

Here is the believer's mistake. Instead of seeking out a thorough way to solve the accusation of conscience, he tries to use other voices to confuse, and even to neutralize, the voice of conscience so as to mitigate its piercing power. The best and easiest way to be liberated from the accusation of conscience is to get rid of that which conscience condemns. In other words, obey God's will in all things. All other means will only deepen a person's rebellion against God.

How many are our explanations! When a believer disobeys God's will, his conscience commences to accuse. What, then, should be done? Explain, reason, argue the why of rebellion? This is one way of bribing the conscience. In so doing, the believer tries to convince himself after he has explained his actions to others as well as to himself that his rebellion against God's will is actually doing God's will. Who realizes that this is absolutely in vain? Nonetheless, the accusation of conscience is hard to bear; and therefore a person loves to devise ways to stifle it. Being unwilling to do God's will, he has to rationalize his rebellion for self-relief so that the sharp sword of conscience may be blunted and he will not be wounded too deeply. Conscience will accuse, but the flesh will not obey. So the device the unwilling believer employs is to use many reasons and much explanation to soothe the conscience, as though saying to the conscience that the present course he takes is not that bad, so why keep on accusing?

Naturally there are other ways to bribe the conscience. Work is one of these ways. In the face of disobedience, a believer will sometimes think of using bigger, better and more works as a substitute for the will of God, as though labor can take the place of doing God's will. Many are the believers who utilize busyness to calm the reproach of their conscience. They are afraid of being still and listening to what conscience may say. For this causes them grief. They are willing to suffer, to labor and to spend and be spent outside of God's revealed will. Their works will so occupy their time that they can safely rebel and reject the correction of their conscience. Even when conscience surreptitiously does say something hard to take, these works become the basis of their answer in bribing their conscience into silence. Are not these works more important? Are they not equally good? Are they not more weighty? Do they not produce more fruit? By their repeating such a litany a number of times, the voice of conscience about a certain issue can hardly be heard. Thus the believers are sheltered in their rebellion against God.

What has heretofore been mentioned is related to the bribing of conscience in large matters. With regard to the hundreds of small things in a believer's daily life, there are also numerous occasions of bribing the conscience. The most common occurrence is the bribing of conscience concerning daily morning Bible reading. Believers will go to their morning work without reading the Bible substantially. How many believers have failed in this matter! Not to read at all grieves the heart of conscience; so a person will merely open the Bible and read but one or two verses. Thus the Bible is "read" in name only; and so the voice of conscience is silenced by using a few verses of the Bible to bribe it and stifle its accusation. Are not the prayers and intercessions of many handled just like this as well? Not to pray at all will disturb conscience. So many believers force themselves to intercede for a few persons and a few matters not unlike the perfunctory calling of the roll at school.

Yet such Bible reading and intercessory prayer are not undertaken for the sake of reading and interceding; rather, they are merely done to bribe the accusation of conscience. Indeed, had conscience not spoken, such reading and intercession would have ceased entirely long ago. But since conscience remains so faithful, it must be reckoned with by believers. And hence, this explains why these casual deeds are undertaken at all—they are done for no other reason than to buy off the conscience.

In the case of many gospel workers, their preaching the message of Christ can likewise be described as perfunctory—and for much the same reason: their conscience must be silenced. Due to dull affection and physical inconvenience, workers can become rather lazy in preaching the gospel. But when faced with sinners who desperately need to be saved, a worker cannot keep his silence long without conscience uttering its habitual accusation. So he reluctantly says a few words of the gospel to them just to bribe his conscience. The word has been preached, duty has been fulfilled, and who, then, can say anything else? Whether or not conscience will still accuse him is now for him a secondary concern. He has employed this superficial action to answer the later reproach of conscience. By performing such crude work he seems to be able to console himself in having fulfilled his ministry. Alas, how deceitful are these self-proclaimed acquittals. Can such so-called gospel work result in God's blessing? How can other people be convicted if the person "preaching" is not convicted himself? As the Bible intimates (see Ps. 125.5-6), there can be no reaping with joy without sowing with tears.

Let me mention one more thing on this entire subject of conscience-bribing. For the latter has a lot to do with what occurs with many believers in the area of their offering and giving. To offer more, the heart is reluctant; yet if *no* offering is made, conscience will not let go of the matter. Thus, the best way to reconcile both these types of actions is to offer a little as a way to bribe one's conscience: an offering has been given, what is required to be done has been done; so now, the believer feels, conscience should not reprove him anymore. Many a time a few pennies of giving has not been done for the reason of loving the poor but merely for the sake of bribing the conscience into silence. As a matter of fact, whenever giving does not cause the heart to ache with joy and the flesh to suffer pain, it cannot be accounted as giving.

These are but a few illustrations. In a believer's life there are numerous occasions when the conscience is bribed. If it is not arguing or reasoning with the conscience it will be some other thing done by the believer as a substitute for the demand of conscience. Such things are multitudinous! This explains much of the reason why believers today are so shallow and have fallen in their spiritual life. Let us not unduly assume that such spiritual condition is due to our lack of Bible knowledge and the knowledge of God's will. I will readily acknowledge that these lacks are present; yet even with our inadequate Scripture knowledge, why do we not listen to the "inner voice"? And even though we are indeed ignorant of God's will in many areas of our lives, we still do not want to obey God in those areas of His will we *are* aware of. Instead, we bribe our conscience as a means of avoidance.

How important it is for us to obey God's will faithfully. Of course, before we can do that, we must first have an honest heart *desire* to do God's will. Without such desire, nothing is of any avail. What we should look for is neither success nor the approval of the world, nor even the peace of conscience; for if our doing God's will is merely to calm conscience, that in itself is already a bribing of conscience. We must see the majesty and greatness of God. Let us do His will solely for the sake of His will. The voice of conscience only indicates where people have gone off the rails from God's appointed path. Unless we live in this world solely for the sake of God's will, how selfish we must be! Do we fear the reproach of conscience more than our rebellion against God? We ought most of all to be fearful of disobeying God's will. How sad that believers live in this world for their own pleasure. For even their obeying God's will is primarily for self-con-solation because they fear their *dis*obeying will bring upon themselves the accusation of conscience, thus causing them to lose their coveted peace and joy. Oh, how very selfish this is! This is none other than the bribing of conscience.

Truly, we must have a new evaluation of God's will and experience a deeper denial of ourselves. We must experience a severe dealing with self-deceit, and a stronger hatred of it. Were a believer to cease from his works of bribing the conscience and commence living daily in God's will, he would see himself in a new heaven and a new earth.